In the name of God

You must read this book

Word by word of this book will capture your soul.

Breath Hold

By

Fatemeh Hashemi

ISBN: 9798338007525

Breath Hold

Dedicated to all:

The girls

And

Boys

Of my land, dear Iran.

Introduction

Stories were written to inform us but, we used them to Sleeping, all of our lives.

Many times, the law is like the law of the Jungle. Because the law writers

Get People wrong with animals.

Law enforcers are only following the written laws. For them only the performance is important, it

Does not matter whether it is right or wrong, in this case, people have to disobey the law to get their

Rights.

A Persian proverb says:

"The head of the innocent goes to the gallows but it does not go to the top of the gallows." I don't

Know who said this wrong Proverb?! I want to strike to this proverb word by word in publics so that

Everyone will understand that it is a lie and thousands of innocent people were hanged and nothing

Happen.

Breath Hold

The law is written by the wolves and the sheep are condemned to be cut

"off to feed the wolves

Cell by cell in my body is like a solitary prison as if I am a prisoner in

myself. Tired of my mood, which is. Like ruin go to the street alone nigh.

Chapter 1

I moved a little on the damp floor, a beam of light shined from the black and dark Ceiling into the

Room. I stared at that light and took a deep breath, I felt nauseous the strong smell of urine burned

My lungs.

The solitary black door opened with a Sound· An iron plate was pushed inside. I was hungry.

I moved my hand to the dish. It was something like chicken food. Tight and Cold. I ate a little but I felt

Nauseous so quickly swallowed it and put a few more in my mouth. I closed my eyes and Swallowed

It and threw the plate to the Corner

I leand against the wall and hugged my legs. It was as if the door and solitary wall were approaching me.

Breath Hold

I felt suffocated. It was as if I was crushed inside the walls and removed. Closed my eyes and

Breathed. Again.... the voice of Nahid echoed in my mind :"Love is a word, but it has a very wide

Meaning. No matter when you start, you will not reach the end. I love you deeply but I can't do anything.

"Even in solitary Confinement, her voice was attractive and it was as hot as hot summer days. I was

Cold and I wanted a cigarette.it was early winter and the ground was cold. A blanket was early in the

Corner of the Cell. I wrapped it around myself. It smelled badly. The smell of vomit, urine, blood lone lines, despair and torture.

Solitary confinement makes the seventh and eighth senses work in addition to the sixth sense

You feel, see, hear things that you cannot feel outside of this wall a thick voice said:

The cell door opened. Blindfold was thrown inside.

Put this in your eyes and come out. I put on blind fold and came out of the narrow Solitary walls. I could feel the tip of the gun on my back.

Guiding me in which way to go he entered room take off your blind fold. I took off room was half lit   there was a table and two chairs in the middle of the room.

I sat on the chair with the gesture of the man who was in the room.

The man was tall and square-shouldered. His face was harsh and his eyebrows were knotted. His hair was bald in front and instead he had a thick, black and long beard he was young, 29 to 30 years old.

"Have you been interrogated before? "His voice was rough and hoarse"

No, I didn't

Have you ever heard interrogation?

I nodded yes.

Suddenly He pulled my hair tightly and while shouting, said:

"You are not having fun here "

Next time, if you answer with your head, I will beat you severely. Do you understand? His Voice was so harsh that, my heart was beating with fear.

I said: yes... understood.

My voice was shaking.

He sat in front of me.

Who ordered you?

What group do you work with?

Who is your leader?

What are your goals?

I stammered:

I… didn't… have... orders… from… any one.

Suddenly, he punched me hard in the face!! Every

Breath Hold

I didn't understand (what they were saying). I didn't cooperate with any group and no gave me orders.

My intention was not murder.

My mount was full of blood and I could not speak properly.

So I spat slowly and said under my breath: about a year ago, my father-in-law, Sadegh Haddad, was arrested and sentenced to death for carring two kilos of drugs.

With cooperation of my brother-in-law we attacked the car of carring the prisoners that we thought were was sadegh in it in order to let him escape.

I got involved with guard Ahamed Rezaee and I shot unintentionally that's all suddenly, he kicked my back and I fell to the ground.

His scream echoed and repeated in the small interrogation room.

Are you telling a story?

I take your word for it, bitch. The sound of his whip echoed in the air and hit my body (it was as if he tore a thousand pieces of my flesh and pulled …..them out with him)again and again

My body was numb. I didn't even feel like moaning.

My body was numb. I didn't even feel like moaning his scream echoed in my ears.

Put his bitch body in solitary confinement.

I don't know low many hours I was unconscious when I woke up I was in solitary confinement. I could hear the puzzling of flies above my head. The smell of blood was so strong that I did not notice the strong smell of urine. I felt numb.

My father's death sentence :I felt numb. Nahids voice echoed in my ears has arrived. Her voice was muffled. I sat next to her and leand against the T wall. I said: I know.

Breath Hold

What should I do now? That damn car was yours.
You knew that there were drugs in that   car. I got
up angrily and shouted. I swear I didn't know.
They were hostile to me. Nahid   also shouted :
why my dad ?

I approached her and while trying to control my
self, I said:

Come and hang me. Nahids tears flowed and she
said in a sad voice: you have to let my father
escape.

Are you crazy?

This is impossible. My daughter Asal was
standing in front of the room and was rubbing her
eyes.

I miss her I forced a smile and opened my arms
for her.

My dear Asal , come to my arms. I hugged her
tightly. I said slowly: tomorrow I will go to the
court and I will take responsibility for everything
Its useless. The only way is to make Dad run
away.

Her eyes were puffy from crying a lot I couldn't stand her crying. I said in a crying voice: I promise you that we will make him escape any way.

Nahid smiled and said: I wish we make decision with our intellect and not with our feelings when making promises some There was moaning. I listened more. The moans got louder. I looked at the ceiling of the cell, there was no light. I realized that it was night. The sound of sound of meaning in creased again. I could even hear the sound of the whip. I wanted to put my hands in my ears so that I could not hear. But my shoulder was hurting. I said to my self sadly: Enough the sell door opened. An Iron plate was pushed inside. I difficulty moved my hand to the plate. It was watery. There was a spoon next to it I ate several spoons in a raw. It smelled like sewage. I tried not to breathe so that the smell would not upset me. suddenly I vomited. What did I sacrifice, Nahid? Sacrifice your old father? I sacrificed my stupidity. Farhad, where are you? Are you listening to me?

Yes….tell me…. Im listening. I bought a gun it is

foldable, its easy to carry.

Breath Hold

Nahid protested: No, Babak ….no gun… no one
was supposed to be killed. Babak said angrily: no
one is going to be killed, but it can't be done
without weapons

My cigarette smoke was too much.

Babak coughed. He opened the window and grunted: you smoke too much, damn you. I really wanted to smoke. My throat was dry It was if my head had become the size of a ton on the cold floor of the cell.

Heavy …. Full of sound. I was terrified by the continuous screams of a woman. Does that mean the womens section is the same as the means?

No it's definitely a man, his voice is thin, Do men scream?

May be I'm hallucinating. A person in solitary confinement hallucinates.

I didn't understand when I slept and when I woke up.

I felt bad I wanted to commit suicide, but I couldn't. The cell door opened.

They blind folded and pushed out.

Again the interrogation and torture room and repeated words again. Probably the person who interrogated me didn't read my dossier or didn't know me. He removed my blind fold.

He was the pervious interrogator.
He sat in front of me and said:" Have you been
punished or are you the same person as before?
I wanted to hit him but my hands were locked he
screamed: I'm with you, bitch.
My hands were locked, but my tongue was not, so
I said in a muffled voice: Do you enjoy cursing
me?
He suddenly hit me in the face with his fist.

I couldn't see any were I felt dizzy and felt the
taste of blood in my mouth. A few moments
passed. I was afraid of his voice.

Breath Hold

Do you work in a group?

Who is the leader of your group?

What's his name?

My lips was torn. I could feel my teeth breaking in my mouth.

I said slowly and hard:

"My wife's father's name is: <<Sadegh Hadad >> with cooperation of my brather-in-law Babak , we wanted to escape him that's all.

He suddenly shouted: mother facker! Haven't you been punished yet?

Komili ……

Someone entered, he was like a giant! His big body scares people. Hang this cuckold.

I don't know how many hours. I was hanging from the ceiling by one foot. What should I say to get them to let me go? I mean is it okey if I say that I work whit a group. They have nothing to do with me anymore. I felt like my brain was coming out of my mouth.

The door opened. It was him again.

He sat right in front of my face.

He said with his thick and scratchy voice:

Look at me.

I looked at him.

He sneered and said:

Are you upset when I swear at your mother?

I didn't say anything.

He suddenly attacked me and pulled my hair.

Hey mother fucker talk to you, answer correctly. Do you understand?

I said slowly: yes…..I understand.

Who is your leader?

Why did you kill the guard Ahamd reza Rezaee?

My jaw hurt, I said with difficulty:

I was working for the hypocrites group.

Our leader's name was Shafagh.

He tore the rope, I fell with my head on the ground.

Breath Hold

Well the rest?

I couldn't speak properly, I didn't have the balance of my mind, so I said: Give me a paper and a pen to write.

Its easer that way. He left the room. I felt a little relieved.

Komili entered the room He lifted me up and I sat on the chair.

He brought paper and pen.

My hand was unable to write I started to write a story with all my strength.

"I am Farhad Fardin I have been working with the group of hypocrites for a few months. Our leader is a 50 year- old man named shafagh. To create fear and terror in the country", we did

I could not think of anything else. I had heard shafaq's name in the news one H be longed to the group of hypocrites. I was not in any group in my life I had nothing to do with politics. But my destiny was that one day I would be accused of politics.

I went back to my cell. High and black solitary wall's again .I fell on the floor. My body was numb I didn't feel the pain sometime I was hot like an oven, then suddenly I was shaking and freezing.

My mom's pleasant voice sounded in my ears: she puts her hand on my head.

How hot you are.   I'm cold. I'm shivering.

You have a cold my dear. She threw the blanket on me.

In solitary cell, you remember big and small memories. As you can live with those memories moment.

Memories that you don't remember in normal times.

Come out of the darkest part of your mind.

When you are in solitary confinement, memories are like breath, air and oxygen.

The blood on my body was still warm. My mouth was full of blood. I tasted, it tasted better than prison food.

There was dried blood around my lips.

I opened the faucet to wash it. I saw a shadow beside me, an me broidered hand kerchief was draw to words me can I help you? I turned to the sound.

Breath Hold

I saw two magical eye's staring at me. I took the hand kerchief

Thank you, m's

My lip was torn and the bleeding would not stop.

I put the hand kerchief on my lip. The smell of her perfume was pleasant.

I know them. Complain about them.

I'm a witness.

Her voice was thin and delicate. She had a special cuteness in her speaking tone that attracted people. When I looked at her. She was beautiful.

I was stunned for a few moments.

She straightened her scarf a little and said confusedly:

I saw your beating and saw that they were bothering you unnecessarily.

There is no need to complain.

I can handle it myself.

A beautiful smile appeared one her lips and she said:

"But you beat them very well".

I said indifferently: what do you want from me?

I saw two magical eye's staring at me. I took the hand kerchief

Thank you, m's

My lip was torn and the bleeding would not stop.

I put the hand kerchief on my lip. The smell of her perfume was pleasant.

I know thcm. Complaiu about them.

I'm a witness.

Her voice was thin and delicate. She had a special cuteness in her speaking tone that attracted people. When I looked at her. She was beautiful.

I was stunned for a few moments.

She straightened her scarf a little and said confusedly:

I saw your beating and saw that they were bothering you unnecessarily.

There is no need to complain.

I can handle it myself.

A beautiful smile appeared one her lips and she said:

"But you beat them very well".

I said indifferently: what do you want from me?

Breath Hold

Suddenly she was
surprised and said: Not…. Nothing ….I just wanted to help you.

She moved bag strap on her shoulder and left without saying good bye.

Because there are many of these girls around me. They fell in love with me as soon as they so my car. I hated this kind of girls.

I went to my car, my body was hurting.

There was 4 of them and I was one. I hit them well, but I was also beaten. My whole body was hurting.

It was summer and was around two ….three in the afternoon.

The street deserted and the weather was very hot. I reached the same girl very soon. She was walking like a loser and dragging her feet one the ground. The strap of her bag was in her.

Fist and sometimes it was dragged on the ground and she went to the said walk.

Girls are strange creatures. If you don't answer their greetings, they think that they have failed in love. "In my opinion, they fall in love quickly and it ends very soon".

My heart burned for her and I braked the

Did I say something funny?!!

While trying to control my laughter, I said:

Na na is a little funny.

She looked annoyed and said:

"well,we say the first letter of our names…….it's easier and stylish this way. For example, my friend's name is Tahere, whom we call ti ti. My other friend's name is Samira, and we call her si si .

I was laughing hard, but I controlled myself any way.

I didn't laugh mostly because my lip was torn.

I raised my eye brows and widened my eyes and said: ooooh! ….. How attractive!

She coquetryly said: Are you kidding me?

I said: No, girls are really creative and they don't make progress inside Iran.

I was laughing in my heart.

I said: in a very serious tone: so, in this case, I will become Fi Fi or Fa Fa.

As if she found something new, she said with a smile:

Yes, your name is Farhad ……that we can say Fi Fi.

The dump girl didn't understand what said herself.

What happened? Why did you brake like that?

I said angrily: how do you know my name? She said easily: is it a crime to know your name?

So, you didn't see my fight by chance and you were following me?

She looked and said: who do you think you are that I follow you?

You are asilly rich baby who shows off with his dad's money. I wanted to throw her out   of the car but controlled myself until she got off herself.

Breath Hold

In the same street were you opened a car exhibition and put expensive cars in it, I rented a small shop and working there. Did to her once she did a lump in her throat.

At first, I wanted to deceive you because you were rich and handsome you.

I looked at you from the window every day until I fell in love with you. The color of your eyes made me crazy and every moment you are in my mind.

I said: I don't like indecent girls.she looked at my eyes and said: why?

Does that mean girls don't have the right to fall in love?

Or like or look and feel? She sighed and said: only you boys have the right? I in differently said: yes …. It has always been like this in our country.

But shouldn't be like that I confidently said: I don't think so. The girl should be modest. A girl who talks about love constantly is not suitable for marriage. After a while she may fall in love with another person. She is not faithful! They cont be good wife or mother. Her lips were bruised because she had bitten them. I'm sorry for your old thoughts.

She said with a crying voice I said mockingly: are you in love with me or my car?

She got angry. Her face turned red like a beet . She opened the door and got out of the car.

She was saying something under her breath. I didn't hear it I think she was saying bad things to me.

I looked at the seat where Nahid was sitting. She had left a black bag. These tricks were old. That dumb girl thought that she left Cinderella's shoes for me to follow her.

But my destiny was something else. The small black old bag became like Cinderella's for me.

The solitary black door

I touched and I couldn't it, it was half cold. I ate a little, it tasted like lentils. I was hungry, so I ate again Damn ! it smelled bad. Nahid, what are we having for dinner?

Adasi. Adasi is not food. She said with a mocking tone: what?! I frowned and said: Adasi is an appetizer. I'm not full with it. I want rice I'm hungry. The sound of moaning and screaming was heared again.

I put my head on the ground. The sound become clearer.

It was the sound of the whipping and moaning it seems is the end of the world. I wish no one would come here.

The red bag was in front of my eyes. Its red color was like the color of blood.

Babak took the bag towards me and said: "the gun is inside it".

Breath Hold

There were two cars I rode xantia and Babak rode peykan. I reviewed everything in my mind. Once ......Twice.....three times....

Thousand times I was confused. I couldn't do it.

We reached the karaj – Qazvin high way

There was a part where cars could go around. We parked there. It was supposed to, a minibus that carring 10 prisoner, pass from here we were told that my father in law"sadegh" was in this car.

Babak pointed to me to be ready. The minibus is coming.

One of his friends was A little ahead and was in forming us. The minibus arrived Babak quickly went to the car and there was a bad sound.

The windows shattered the minibus stopped. I took the gun and put on my mask and got into the minibus. The prisoner's officer was in the car He was confused. Once he become conscious and took out his gun. But it was too late.

I was completely on top of him.

I shouted, put down you gun.

He hesitated a little I fired two aerial shots. Everyone was scared and screaming. I was more scared than others my hands were shaking. Babak was supped to enter behind me, but he didn't come.

On the officer's uniform was writhe"rezaee".

He threw his gun on the ground. I shouted again: lie down quickly and he lay down. I was still waiting for Babak but there was nothing going on him. I was very scared I looked at all the prisoners car.

The bottom of the gun was in my hand and the barrel was in guard Rezaeis hand.

I didn't want him to get hurt, and tried to pull the gun out of his hands. It was ready to fire suddenly I shot unintentionally: pass yar Rezaei fell on the ground. There was blood everywhere I couldn't believe that I had killed a person. I was shocked. Xantia was approaching me and the sound of Babaks scream took me out of shock.

Harry Farhad …. The officers coming now….. Get in the car. I got to the car and we ran away.

That day, the Karaj- Qazvin high way was closed for 5 hours and there was a terrible traffic jam.

The heart-rending death of guard Ahamdreza Rezaei was published in media very soon.

The first head line of the newspapers was about the martyrdom of Ahamadreza rezaei. Alot of this news was published with exaggeration. "T

"The killer already knew the victim",

"The killer was a hypocrite" ,

"The killer was one of the enemies of the regime",

The killer was directed from outside Iran"

"The killer came from the Musat group from Israel to create insecurity".

"The killer had orders from the great enemy, American, to terrorize and create anger. Police officers were still at the scene.

There was no more traffic.

Investigator Islami wrote the result of his investigator as follows:

"The accident was fake, the perpetrators did it with a previous plan. The "paykan" car left there is a good clue and will lead us to the killer."

Breath Hold

A special team of expert criminal detectives from Alborz and Tehran were present there and they were responsible for handing it. Investigator.

I slami was a tall, imposing "square- shouldered and charismatic man. He had many medals that hanging on his clouds. He walked and spoke proudly.

His full, black and knotted eye brows made him more imposing or even more frightening. The balls of his eyes were like black coal.

He had special face and voice that remained in the mind.

He had a special mastry over his subordinates. He pointed with his hand and 4 person immediately approached him.

The 4 of you must find the owner of "paykan" by tomorrow morning with a movement of his hand he emphe size and said: only buy tomorrow morning.

Do you understand? All four people showed military respect and left. Alborz court judge.

Mr. momeni told the propaganda forces: inform the martyr's father "guard Ahamdreza Rezaei" that the funeral will not be held tomorrow. An order has been received from the higher authorities to notify all small and large cities.

On Friday after the "Friday prayer ,"(Jumu'ah) the funeral is performed. On Tuesday morning, a tin man of about fifty years old, small in stature, with his hands tied, was in the office of" Islami"

Investigator sir…. The owner of"paykan" is this man the investigator shouted angrily: Hy idiot ….. This mortal man is good for nothing. He walked around the room with a little anger and said to the security guard "Falahi":

Tell me his information …..Who is he?

What is his job? ….. Was he driving or not? It dose not fit his body to hold a gun.

Guard Falahi paid his respects and said: according to his statements and our research, he sold the car to a person named "kourosh jazayeri" a week ago. Of course, the cars is still in his name.

The investigator said to the man: "why did you sell the car?

The man, who still does not know the manner and character of the investigator, calmly shrugged (his thin and bony shoulders) and said:

Breath Hold

Well, I needed its money.

Once, the investigator screamed in anger: The sound of the glass shaking was clearly heard.

Buster!....I order you to be hanged from the ceiling to die. Answer correctly.

The man's bones were shaking from fair His wrinkled skin was morning up and down on his body.

His eyes were round with fear.

He said in a trembling and choked voice: I swear to god, I needed money.

The investigator asked sternly: who was he? What was his name?

His friend call him kuorosh he said that his last name was jazayeri ....or jazirai.......or I don't know .... It was jozam.

Do you have any evidence about him?

A copy of brith certificate ......or telephone number......? No

The investigator threatened, " pray that we find this guy otherwise I will order you to be hanged.

The man was very scared and glared at the investigator.

Suddenly a feeling of courage rose in him and he recklessly said:" I work hard from morning to night ......I don't want to stay alive for a long time, if you order me to be hanged, you have done me a great favor.

Poverty and wretchedness were evident on his face.

It's as if a layer of skin has been stretched over several pieces of bone The investigator had calmed down and told the guard.

Fallahi:" take him to the face painting section and then keep him in the detention center.

Yes sir. This time, in a stronger voice:

He said to Fallahi before sunset, any one with the name of kuorosh jazayeri, or

Jozani in Tehran or the suburbs should be in my room.

Fallahi was standing and listen the investigator shouted: Fallahi, I'm with you……

Did you understand? Poor guard Fallahi quickly said: Yes sir…….I understood.

Tell them to provide you a special team. Yes sir Fallahi went out with the owner of peykan. He said to the man : what was your name? " Tavana", my name is Tavana Eskandari" Fallahi grinned and said slowly: how well his name suits his body!(Tavana means capable).

He paused and said again: Mr. Eskandari if you want to get out of here, pay attention in the face drawing section Mustache, beard, eye color, skin and hair, hairy or bald, age, atc.

Pay attention to all.

Breath Hold

Tavana's nose is running. He wiped it with his sleeve and said:

My body needs drugs, give me some drugs so I can co

Glass and morphine are simple things.

They arrived in front of the face painting room. Falahi call out:

GHolami?

A young man about 25-26 years old carne forward.

Yes ……?

Tavana was handed over to you.

Then he said more slowly: the case is handled by the higher authorities and it is very sensitive. Make sure that the face is identified well.

Gholami agreed Falahi went near.

Gholami and said more slowly: take a strang drug and give it to Tavana for better cooperation him.

Tavana was sitting in front of the computer and several members of face painting were next to him.

Make his mustache brown.

Is it good?

Make it a little smaller. His hair was thin. In front of his head was a little bald, but he had a pony tail at the back of his head that looked like a rat's tail is it.

Good……..?

Yes…..

I will talk to Islami investigator.

Tavana was excited and kissed Gholami firmly. His cheek bones were very visible on his face I was not clear from addiction or hunger.

Tavana looked at monitor and said:

His body was athletic

Salami said: we don't have anything to do with his figure.we only focus on his face.

Sajadi said: was his face round or elongated? Was he chubby or thin?

Tavana put his hand on his face and said: yes he was thin … but … no……

He was normal… he wasn't chubby, he wasn't skilny…….yes…..yes……he is becoming like himself.

Gholami said:

Tavana, concentrate, what other characteristi did he have?

A mole…..a knife mark …..Wasn't there anything special on his face?

Once, Tavana said:

I think he was a very important person.

Tavana looked at the people and said

Breath Hold

Salami said:

What do you mean?

Tavana scratched his wrinkled skin and said:

I mean this guy who was killed must have been an important person that everyone is looking for.

Gholami said: Finally, someone has been killed and the killer must be found.

Tavana wailed and said:

Come to Harandi I live there.

Salami said: is your house there??

No one has a home there ….. Everyone lives, sleeps and takes drugs on a piece of card board. There, every morning when you wake up some people die.

He took a deep breath and said: in muffled.

Voice: no one asks us how we are? .... No one says these people die?

Did they die of hangover? No one asks who is the killer?

Sometimes they stay there for a long time until their corpses blow up, then people come and take them away.

Gholami and salami just watched. Basically, they didn't have any answer to say, may be they were afraid to say anything.

Sajadi said:

They are waiting for someone to be shot. Then call him a "martyr" and advertise otherwise, the person himself is not important to them. He wants to be an important person or not.

Only the word "martyr" is important to them.

They need the name of "martyr" because they rule with this name, because the foundations of their system are attached to this word.

Gholami gave him a sharp look and said: shhhhh! Are you crazy?!

The sun had not set yet. About 50-60 people had forcibly gathered outside the room of major islami.

Everyone was looking for the name kuorosh with the last name of Jazayeri, Jazeeri or Jozani. Some were scared and some were grumbling but no one knew why they were here. Everyone said somting: I passed the red light yesterday.

They must have brought me here for the same reason. Well, I will pay the fine.

Another one said in a muffled voice:

I posted a political post yesterday, I think that's why I'm here.

The person next to him looked at him looked at him and said:

I stole someone's mobile phone yesterday. That must be the reason. Those around him were looking at him angrily and cursing a young man of about 25-26 years old, who had tattoos on his arms and had his hair up like a cocks crown, loudly said:

We are all here only because of our name.

The name of everyone who is here is "kuorosh". Onetime there was a riot

One said:

What d

Breath Hold

Another one who was almost old, said:

It has been a crime to go to passargad (the tomb of kuorosh) for many years. Anyone who goes will be arrested another one.

Who was obviously every scared said:

Well, they were announcing earlier that we were changing our names.

Another one said:

I swear to God my name is kuorosh on the birth certificate everyone calls me Ali.

Another one said in the said with a trembling voice: Ayatollah Khomeini said in the first days that: "Iran's 2500 years empire was a disgrace and we should have changed our name"

At the same time Tavana was brought in for facial recognition for the first time, he felt strong.

The Islami investigator came in and several people showed military respect he looked confused and nervous he said to Tavana in a hoarse voice:

"Look well......maybe he has changed his face".

Once someone said in a loud voice and in a contemptuous tone:

"Should this addict recognize the face? I'm suing you the Islami investigator clenched his teeth and shouted angrily:

Falahi, put this bastard in the detention center. If he dose it again, send him to Evin prison. Falahi obeyed the man was still shouting when he suddenly felt a gun on his temple the man who had a gun said slowly: shut your mouth until I shoot.

The man become silent all voices were silenced not even the sound of their breathing could be heard Tavana looked carefully at the faces.

No…..

He isn't ….

No……

He isn't ……

He isn't ……

The Islami investigator was very angry. He was holding the photo that was obtained in the face painting, and he was looking at the faces one by one.

Falahi…..?

Yes sir…….?

They can all go.

Yes sir.

We gave the system a picture drawn with the help of Tavana.

Breath Hold

A person named Babak Hadad, about 30 years old, looks like this photo once the investigator shouted: Its him…… its definitely him.

Gholami trembled at the scream of the investigator.

The investigator asked: does he have a history?

About 5 years ago, he had a bounced check…..he was imprisoned for 2 months The hall was deserted everyone had left the hall very quickly and without protest

No one dared to ask why he was here you brought us here with force, pressure and guns and now. You are saying to leave they didn't even give a simple a pology.

The Islami investigator said to Falahi:

Babak Hadad's case will be on my desk in 5 minutes yes sir.

He said again with more authority:

I want this man until the end of tonight find him wherever he is hiding until tonight, do you understand?

Yes sir.

Caption Falahi paid military respect and left.

Nahid has not heard from Farhad and Babak since yesterday their mobile phones were not available she was suffocating from worry I ghorance is the worst and the most painful feeling in the world she went to her father's house with her doughter " Asal"

Ever since her father was carring 2 kilos of crack and glass, his mother had also become ill and stress and bad news made her condition worse that's why they hid the news from her Nahid hoped to find news about Farhad and Babak at her father's house.

It was winter, but it was a strange winter it wasn't snowing or raing , but the weather was cold.

It was early at night Nahid looked at the street lights, they were all off she said to herself: curse these lights that are always off she reached the alley of his father's house there was a commotion in her heart there was a car parked in the alley.

It was on Nahid felt that someone was looking at her from inside the car there was 3 or 4 men in the car she said to herself: I hate nosy and ide people.

Alley wasn't like usual she reached the house and took out the key her hands was shaking she put the key in the door. A person in black approached her what do you have to do with this house? His voice was loud and thick.

Nahid was scared and she was holding Asal.

To herself she looked at the man he was tall and square shouldered the color of his clothes was dark and he had small eyes

Nahid felt a slight tremor inside her, but she tried to be firm and strong she wanted to say: it doesn't concern you.

But she couldn't and stammered: I…..

Breath Hold

Do you know where is he?

Nahid said with difficulty " No"

And went inside the house she dragged her feet on the ground and walked. Her heart was beating hard Asal was scared she looked at her mother's pale face and said:

Mom…..what's wrong,mom?

Nahid said to herself: I must not let Babak get arrested ……I must let him escape anyway she said to Asal:

You go to grandma she opened the door and came out.

Suddenly in the middle of the alley the sound of gun shouts rang out in the air she saw that her only brother was hand cupped end thrown into the car.

Nahid was crying silent and staring at Babak she was nauseous and dizzy

She muttered to herself:

Why……why couldn't I do something?

Sometimes it happens like this you just have to watch and cry.

Sometimes it's not the way you want. Sometimes…….sometimes you just have to watch and not talk Babak hadn't reached the detention center yet, but he was very scared I swear to God …..I didn't shoot ……I…..I….I didn't kill anyone.

Major Falahi said: how many people were there? What are their name and addresses? The name and addresses of person who shot? Where is he now?

It didn't take an hour for Major Falahi and his group along with Babak Hadad to find Farhad and arrest him.

Breath Hold

Chapter: 3

The door was opened an iron plate was pushed inside it
smelled very bad.

I was used to the smell I reached in to the plate and put some in my mouth.

It tasted like old flour may be it was Halva , but it wasn't sweet. I was sure that
cattle would not eat his food.

But I'm worthless here than cattle. Am I human?!........Am I man or woman?!
...........Am I a live or dead?!............I shouted once:

Get rid of me……….please execute me………..shoot me.

My voice echoed in the cell a few seconds later, they threw a blind fold inside put on the blind fold, you have to go to the interrogation.

I was afraid of the interrogation I begged:

Please……I will say whatever you want ……don't take me for interrogation.

They didn't care, I went to the interrogation room by force and with a gun. I sat on the chair, removing my blind fold, the interrogator was sitting in front of me.

I wanted to die at that moment his voice was hurting my soul.

So……….tell me compeletly…….what's the name's.

Of your group mates where is the address of your headquarters?

Who is your boss?

What are you goals?

His voice was very harsh.

Breath Hold

Word by word, his words hit me like a whip. I said with fear:

Our boss's name was " shafaq" we did this to creat fear you said these things of your headquarters?........

Where did you gather? ....

I gave the address of a basement where my father had a production work shop.

Several years ago and it was now abandoned I also mentioned some unrealistic names: Hossein Zangi.......

Mahmoud Panahi...........

Mohammad Iftekhari...........

Hassan Tajik..........

Once he pulled my hair and said: if the names and address are in correct.

Its bad for you. I knew he wasn't lying ....what could I say to make him leave me.

I went back to my cell the smell of cigarettes was coming from outside I wanted to smoke.

I closed my eyes and took a deep breath and swallowed all the smell of cigarettes Farhad..........I hate the smell of cigarettes........

I feel sick......go to the terrace and smoke I frowned and said:

I like to lie on the coach and smoke. She came to me and took the cigarette and said: " cigarette, means cancer ....don't smoke anymore " I got angry and yelled:

Nahid ....your behavior was very unpleasant. Nahid smiled artificially and said:

" Well, I hate the smell of cigarettes" I grinned and said:

Why does your father smoke all kinds of drugs, don't you feel bad?!

She also shouted and said: that's my dad ....I can't tell him anything.

I exploded with anger and shouted at the top of my voice:

Damn you, I am also your husband you have no right to say anything ……do you understand?…….

I came out of the house now I understand what "respect" means?

What dose "politeness" means?

What dose "culture" means?

Now, I understand tood the meaning of this proverb better my mother always respected my father "Birds of feather, folck to gethe" But Nahid didn't know how to respect her husband. She didn't speak politely she bothered me with his behavior.

I loved Nahid but our culture and up bringing were different once.

I felt Asal's voice coming ………my dear father I hugged her.

My whole being was filled with love the wounds caused by the whip didn't burn on my body any more the cold and black walls of my cell didn't bother me.

I hugged her tightly I wanted to live …….to live my beautiful honey-eyed girl.

Nahid frowned and said:

Do you like honey colored eyes?

I was surprised by his question my eyes were honey too.

I said: no, it doesn't mather……because they are the same colore as my eyes.

I fell good she shrugged her shoulders indifferently and said:

"But the colore of black eyes is much more beautiful and special from her childish jealously I laughed I smiled and said:

Of course it is Its clear that you are more special, my dear I paused a bit and said mischievously:

Breath Hold

your eyes made me fall in love with you she smiled approached me and said doubtfully:

Are you serious, Farhad?..........

I raised an eye brow and said: have I ever lied? She wrapped her hands around my neck and said:

No …..not at all ………

We all laughed together we were so happiness tears flowed from the corners of my eyes damn the past …….. My past.

Brought me here today is the sixth day that I was imprisoned in this hell hole the dog house is bigger than here the strong smell of excrement was bothering my lungs.

The buzzing sound of hundreds of files was disturbing my nerves the small solitary window was opened the gurd's head entered and said in his thick voice.

"Tomorraw at 10 o clock in the morning it's your court turn".

Prepare yourself I was happy at least I would get rid of this hell for a few hours I couldn't breath properly any more there was no oxygen.

Here I put my head on the ground, as if I was going to fall I felt that the rope was pressing on my neck:

My body was suspended in the air and was moving here and there I was dying.

My face was bruised and I wanted air…….air……air……

Suddenly the sound of successive screams and moans intensified and became louder I lifted my head from the ground and put it between my legs and pressed the moans were getting louder and louder I could hear the sound of the whip and when it came down the moaning became louder. I felt that they were whipping me along with the sound of screams and moans, I wailed and cried.

Where are the people who defend human rights now?

Why don't they pay attention to us?

Where is the law? Where is the justice?

I remembered my father's words: this country is not governed by the law be careful don't do anything that will force you to take help from the law.

It was the middle of the night……… I was sleeping ………the cell door opened and someone pushed in…….I was confused ………who is this?! My brain was not working……..!

Hi bro…….My cell was dark and I couldn't see his face, there was so little space that we were tied together.

I quickly asked him: who are you?

Why did you come here It's too small for me.

I killed people just like you ……. I take money and killed people. I didn't say anything ………I was scared and his manner of speaking was like women.

He said again: My bro ………I have killed more than 10 people so far ……..and once he laughed and giggled ……….!

I said under my breath:

Breath Hold

I protested: can you not be so close to me?

Suddenly he put his hand inside my pants! I quickly hit his hand and yelled:

Hey ……….son of a bitch! What are you doing?

He quickly put his hand under my throat………I felt something sharp I was very scared and didn't move.

Tomarrow in the court, say you have a hypocrite and you had orders from America to make Iran un safe ………..to create terror ………do you understand? I was afraid to shake my head, the tip of the razor had split the skin of my throat and was burning. I said slowly:

Ok………I understand he took the bald from under my throat and started yelling: the door opened the guard asked:

What's wrong? He said with voice that was like the buzzing of a fly's wings:

This bastard wanted to rape me……

He has a knife and wanted to do it by force ………

The guard insulted me I couldn't say anything ……..

I couldn't even defend myself …….I hate myself. I always thought I was a brave man. Its time like this that you realize how brave you are. Prison and torture make you coward. That's when I realized that I have to take
responsibility for everything my life was sacrificed.

Chapter: 4

I was in court at 10 am. It was crowded several reports were wating with cameras.

The public prosecutor and the revolution of

This murder was committed by a person named Farhad Fardin how is now in court this murder was planned by the enemies of Islam to threaten Iran's national security, and this case has been proven by the court and the murder. When the prosecutor's speaking finished, it was my turn to go to the stand we ask mr. Farhad Fardin to come to the stand and make his last defense. I didn't know why I should go there Dose that meanI really have the right to defend myself? The judge said: you are accused of murdering the security guard Ahamad reza rezaei. If you have a defense of yours self, tell us I looked at the audience, but I didn't see Nahid or any acquaintances or relatives I wanted to know is Babak........?

Is he in prison or free? I wanted to know if these disasters that happened to me, happened to him or not? I wanted him to be imprisoned and tortured like me, why only me?

But I wanted him to be free and at least one man would take care of Nahid and my doughoter

Asal.

In this cruel world, if a woman is alone she will definitel get hurt I saw my father for a moment how old he was my heart burned for him and it broke in to thousands of pieces I was on the verge of tears I said to myself: you are going to be executed, don't let them execute you as a spy or a hypocrite. Now speak up don't let your father get upset more that this. I looked around the court.

Reporters ....consultants ....prosecutors-lawyers ....and all those I didn't know But my father's presence encouraged me.

I looked at the audience and then at the judge and said:

Breath Hold

Honorable judge ……..audience…….counselors……..reporters………..I have been told to come here and confess that I am a hypocrite and I cooperate with a group of hypocrites.

I had to say that I'm taking orders from the enemies of Iran and Islam in prison and under torture, I falsely confessed to all this I paused and took a deep breath and said in louder voice: I confess here in front of everyone that I am not a hypocrite and I don't cooperate with any group I admit that I killed a young man named Ahamad reza Rezaei, but I had no personal enmity with him I didn't know him at all honorable judge ……….my father –in-law was sent enced to death for carrying 2 kilos of drugs.

The drugs were embedded in my car I don't know, who did this?……..why and for what reason?

I don't know, but my life was destroyed we just wanted to escape my father-in-law that day.

My brother-in-law "Babak Hadad" was also with me. I swear to God that our intention was not insecurity and murder.

I swear I didn't shoot the shot was fierd unintentionally and it was an accident when I looked at my father, I became more courageous and raised my voice involuntarily: I risked for my life I am human being and I made a mistake to save my life I was on the verge of tears, saying: they call me "killer" I don't know how the killer is defined in the law book?

But I can't kill even an ant now. There are those who commit crimes and murder, but they don't care and the law has nothing to do with them everyone was silent. It was as if they were influenced by my words I begged : I am still young and I want to live.

The guard Rezaei's father disturbed the silence of the court by shouting he is a murder, he should hanged in public.

I myself will hang the rope around his neck and count the moments for that day.

The court was crowded for a few moments I was giving him the right he had lost his son but I didn't do it on purpose he persisted I wish that bullet had hit me there was silence a gain and I returned to my place the judge said: Mr. Ehsani the lawyer of Farhad Fardin, com to the place my father must have a gotten a lawyer for me.

It's good that I had this right at least Mr. Ehsani went to the stand he was tall and his belly was slightly bulging and he had little hair in front of his head. He was in middle years and it suits him to be a capable lawyer.

Breath Hold

After greeting the audience and expressing his condolences to the Rezaei's family, Mr. Ehsani said: I will start my defense with this sentence from the holy prophet: "If thousands of guilty people are free, Its better than the innocence of punishment or be executed"

I appeal to the honorable judges of the supreme court, who are all first-class scholars andne clerics of the holy seminary, to make a decision with more know ledge and certainty and issue a verdict my client, Mr. Farhad Fardin is a 30-years-old young man how, in order to save his life, did a great stupidity that unintentionally led to the martyrdom of guard Ahmad reza Rezaei, my client isn't of the evildoers, hypocrites or enemies and he dose not ocooperate with any group or gang he is an ordinary man who has never been imprisoned by chance or in other words, his bad luck has caused him trouble in this case I request from the guard Rezaei's honorable father, who is one of the dear.

Teachers of our country, that ……..suddenly the court was in chaos It was crowded the sound of wailing, crying, cursing and shouting filled the court.

Suddenly, the order of the court was disrupted it was crowded the sound of wailing. Crying, cursing, and shouting filled the courtroom the voice of the prosecutor was heart loud and clear: this court session is enough to deal with Mr. Farhad Fardin's accusations and it will not be renewed next week, the verdict of murderer will be issued and it will not be contested in any way the flash of cameras hits my eyes, they think that arrested a serial killer!

Although the great murderers are never arrested we are common people who are tried in his way every one notices our execution so that no one notices the great murderers and their crimes I was looking for my father with my eyes I saw him crying I cried and my tears rolled down my face.

I wish I would die and not see my father in this state I wanted to be allowed to hug him for a moment "But I was deprived of everything and condemned to everything".

They took me straight to the interrogation room again, the whip ….whip
and the harsh voice of the interrogator, scares me.

Breath Hold

Why didn't you say in court that you are with the enemies of the regime? Why didn't you say that you cooperate with the group of hypocrites? Why ………..why………why………?

When I peel you skin, you will know I wished to die and get rid of it. I couldn't bear to be tortured anymore it was as if I was surrounded by wolves, but wolves have more honor than humans the wolf has mercy on its kind, but not humans! In my land you must be a wolf. Love, life sacrifice, mistake and compensation have no meaning here humanity is meaning less here I was lying on the floor in the cell and was shaking I was terribly afraid of the world "inrerrogator".

I wanted to beg them to execute me they will execute me with any name and title they like I begged under my breath: I'm what ever you say I couldn't remember begging anyone in my life I didn't even know what begging means?

But in this small and dark cell, my whole being was full of begging damn you …..tell me who should I beg?!

Chapter: 5

I was lying on the bed and smoking today I entered the general ward of the prison I was in solitary confinement for two months I had become a different person, I felt that I had become a stranger to myself who am I ?!........ what did I do to myself?!.......... sometimes I believe that I was a dangerous person. Can you give me a cigarette my bro?

His voice was black familiar he sounded like a woman.

Breath Hold

I looked at him, he was black, thin and old I recognized him from his voice he came to me in solitary confinement then he screamed and said that I was going to assault him!

He saw that I was looking at him what is it bro?.........

Tell me I don't have ……..why are you looking like this? I was afraid to say something I just said: I don't have it his face made me feel load as well as his voice the sentence was of my execution had been issued the sentence was final and I had no right to protest Ahmad reza Rezaei's father had protested against this sentence and said that I should be execution was delayed ……..what is your name?

He sat next to me ………I liked his voice He was a bout twenty five years old with thin and elongated face he had big eyes I said in hoarse voice:

Farhad Fardin what a beautiful name! I forced a smile ………what is your crime? Murder …….. his big eyes become rounder and he asked: so why you did get put in the political prison? I paused I was afraid to talk too much It's true that I was sentenced to death, but it was worse than executed a thousand times, I will not go to solitary confinement again I looked at him his look give peace I said: I killed a guard has the ruling been issued?

I took a deep breath that was full of pain and said: execution he said under his breath I'm sorry.

It's easy to hear the word "execution", but it's very difficult for someone like to say it. It seems that every single letter of this word kills a person all out of the mouth, it squeezes your throat until you die, but eventually it releases you.

If you have something to do, tell me my name is Mikael I agreed with the movements of my head I didn't feel like talking : I lay down I wanted to smoke a gain and remembered my me mories a gain my son, this girl's bag has been is your room for a few days.

Your father will be upset if he sees it you know he doesn't like these things for a few days, there was a small black flaky bag on the corner of my desk I remembered that girl I smiled and said: I don't know the owner of the bag.

It means …….it is for a girl she got in to my car and left he bag my
           mother frowned and said sadly: these thing aren't right.

Breath Hold

I couldn't explain everything to her it was better not to say anything mom left the room I wanted to throw the bag out, but I couldn't maybe there was something important in it money or documents I put the things inside the bag on the table.

The smell of perfume inside it filled the room there was a small fragrance between the items I took it under my nose.

It smelled amazing! I looked at the rest of her thing lipstick ……..red nail polish black eye pencil…a small mirror …..

Keychain…..flash drive………CD…..note book……a small package around it was wrapped with tape I got curious and opened it.

It was like a few bird bones! I didn't understand what it was ………I called my mom. What? …….. what happened?………. look, what is this ?!

My mom looked at me and the bag and then said: you had no right to open the bag I was looking for a phone number or an address to return the bag to her.

Pointing to the opened package, I said: what is this?! It was packed very tightly my mother looked carefully and then laughed and said: these are the bones of the spain of a snake some girls believe that these bones bring them luck that's why they put it in their bag I raised my eye brows and said in surprise: wow! We both laughed my mother pointed with her hand and said: put it in her bag and left the room thinking that I would find her number, I opened her note book in the first page was a painted picture I looked carefully…….

How similar it was to me! I was painted more beautiful than myself!
Under the photo it was written in a beautiful hand writing : "in the name of love, I swear to love I swear to your name, my Farhad".

I swear by honey which is the same color as your beautiful and charming eyes, my Farhad. Really …… my heart trembled "God………I'm begging you all your world is for others but Farhad is my world, I don't want him to be for anyone else.

The next page was written :"I love you my Farhad for ever ….. Sometimes missing your honey colored eyes is the craziest feeling in the world". I no longer felt the small tremors of my heart.

I felt tremors like an earthquake inside me!!! Like an earthquake ……….I could feel the heat from all her hand written words.

I read her writing word by word, letter very carefully I turned to the next page: " you are the drop …..you are the sea………you are the anger ……you are the poison …….don't bother me anymore ……

Next page: " I write Farhad………..Farhad………Farhad……..I put a pin an my heart and it starts beating".

Next page: " No matter what I do, you will not leave my heart I avoid you, but I see you in front of me again".

Next page: "I love you, my Farhad ….. Beyond all the borders of the world".

Next page:" Your eyes drive me crazy." I felt that I have been in love for years. I tried to remember her face but I didn't! It wasn't important Its important to know that someone loves you to the point of madness.

That's when you fall in love a pleasant and loving warmth filled my entire being how easy and silent love came! I didn't understand how it came! It is said that love and filling in love is complicate, but I say it is simple.

It is the easiest thing in the world I fell in love with a few words.

Breath Hold

Someone waved me once getup.......lunch is over now it was mikaeil's warm and beautiful voice.

I went to the dining room with him there was iron and black dishes on top of each other I took one and went forward he poured two spoon fuls of food the color of the water was dark and black there was something like overcooked peas and beans in the food and it smelled bad it was as if they had made it with sewage water I sat next to Mikaeil and forcefully ate a spoonful damn it smells like shit. Mikaeil looked at me and said:

You're getting used to it I said under my breath: I 'm not getting used to it they give me the same food in solitary confinement he put some food in his mouth with the tip of a spoon, then closed his eyes and swallowed so........ you were in solitary confinement for 2 months I said in a choked voice: yes.

So were you tortured? I took a deep breath the thought of torture tormented me. I said: I was tortured in every way.

Mikaeil said: talk, it makes you not understand the taste of food I swallowed a few spoonfuls and then asked : are you also a political prisoner?

That's what they say I asked with surprise: what's your crime? I 'm Bahai what dose it mean?! That is my crime is that I am a Bahai I said with annoy once: if you don't like it, don't say it, I don't insist. Mikaeil put his hand around my neck.

He said with a said voice there is Iran……… Religion is compulsory" Being a Bahai in Iran means being an enemy of religion and system Bahai means you are a disbeliever and war with the infidel is part of the law of the Islamic republic of Iran.

It was hard for me to believe it! I asked in surprised: does that mean you were imprisoned because you are a Bahai?! Ether we have to hide our Bahai status or we have to accept prison and sometimes execution the bad taste of the food remained in my mouth I felt better with a glass of water we passed through the narrow corridor It was so narrow that we could walk hardly there were 4 cells in the corridor about 50-60 people were hardly fit in these cells there were 14-15 people in each cell. We returned to our cell I was cold I pulled a blanket over myself it smelled bad.

Mom………this blanket smells

Because you smoke a lot she took the blanket put another one on me I coughed my mother said sympathetically: don't smoke so much, my son it's not because of smoking mom, I have a cold she puts her hand on my fore head yes….. How hot!.........let's go to the clinic I will go tomorrow my mother went out grumbling why don't you take care of yourself?

Why don't you wear warm clothes? I took Nahid's note book again I needed her writings.

I opened it she had written: my Farhad, you make me feel calm without you the day and the night is no different for me.

Breath Hold

My Farhad, seasons and years are no different without you when my love doesn't feel in his heart, my heart is as sad as the world little by little ……….my lover's heart is dying without you, my Farhad, my Farhad ………without you, life id death for me I had a fever and my body was shaking because of a cold I was in a very bad mood. Farhad I love you without permission.

Eyes from you, tears from me heart from you beat's from me if there is death it's from me I was in a strange mood I read each word and sentence hundreds of times I put the note book on my face and cried it smelled like love I said under my breath: I want you ……whoever you are…I will find you wherever you are I opened her perfume I smelled and enjoyed it I unconsciously put it on my lips, also on my face and cheeks.

I had a fever I felt something sharp on my throat I quickly stood up he was one of my cell mates with the tip of the spoon he had sharpened he pressed my throat.

I asked with fear: what is it ……. What do you want this is my place go and sleep on the floor his voice was thick why his voice got louder: are you blind?

There isn't enough space ……. You have to sleep on the floor.

I looked at the floor several people were sleeping on the floor of the cell it was cold and it was the middle of winter I spread a blanket on the floor and lay down and put a thin blanket on myself the blanket smelled very bad it was as if they had vomited on it was very dirty my body was itchy and infested with lice they turned off all the lights and the cell was silent after a few days, I realized that all the prisoners in ward 7, where I was there were not political there are some financial convicts, some for buying and selling drugs, and some for murder but most of them were political prisoner I found out very soon that there are too many people with AIDS and hepatitis inside the prison although it didn't matter for me who was sentenced to death for me there was the end of the world.

I was heartbroken I came to the door of the cell and stared at the narrow corridor I lit the cigarette that Mikeil had given me I heard that your death sentence was issued…….I turned to the sound an old man was around 60-70 years old.

The hair on his head his beard and mustache his eye brows and even his eye lashes were white he had a bony and thin face I didn't say anything how good you will be comfortable his words stressed me out how can someone be so disgusted with life?!

I left bad for him although I needed more pity myself I was at the end of the line I asked: what's your crime? I killed 2 people what sentence did they give you life imprisonment.

I asked in surprise: why life imprisonment?!

Why didn't they give the death sentence?! Will you give me the end of your cigarette?

I gave cigarettes were like gold in prison of course, for those who had money everything was available: cigarettes opium crack and glass everything was available for them people like me who were not allowed to visit didn't even get money.

Breath Hold

She was a few years younger than me we were partners in the shop and we had a fruit shop a few monthes had passed since our marriage when the war started the old man took a breath and said: I told my wife that I have made my decision the enemy has attacked my home land.

I must go to war and defend my country my wife cried and said: if something happens to you I will die I can't live without you I said: trust in God my brother also wanted to participate in the war but my mother didn't allow him and said: only one of you can go I was captured at the beginning of the war in captivity.

All my happiness was thinking about her with the hope of Soheila I endured the hard days and nights of captivity I was released after 10 years he kept silent for a while …….as if it was difficult for him to say tears gathered in his eyes " Bitter memories always live with people until they destroy the moments."

I returned to my home land with great pleasure and prid I wish I never came back I wish I would die in captivity or be killed in war my wife was married to my brother they said: they thought I was as killed so easy …… but I was alive and they had a wedding party.

They had two children! Those days were bad very bad my mood was very bad I was unhappy and upset with everyone I couldn't bear it anymore I bought a colt and killed both of them then I went straight to the police station and surrendered a tear slipped down in his face he slowly said: curse the war ………

I said to myself: curse the war ……… curse the bullet ……….curse the cruelty……..cruse the endless stupidity of mam kind.

Chapter: 6

It was time to sleep …..I was still sleeping on the floor of the cell I couldn't sleep and I was tossing from one side to the other in my bed I wanted to smoke there was a sound and the door opened with a small knock I saw my mother's kind face she said worriedly: "Its half the night, why don't you sleep, my dear?"

I was sitting by the window and smoking she sat next to me and said in low but kind voice: "Your smoking kills me.

Breath Hold

I said with annoyance: God forbid………. Don't say that I extinguished half of the cigarette

And threw it out the window she stared at me…… is something wrong.

My dear you've been upset for a while, what's wrong? Did you argue with your father? It was as if I was waiting for such a word ……..I said: I want to get married. My mother was surprised and said in disbelief : "with whom?"

Her name is Nahid well ……what dose "well" mean?

It means: who are her family? Do we like them or not? Because I didn't know her I said very brief

Briefly: well……. She is a good girl and loves me very much ……… she said again:

Tell about her family and her parents do we know them it was clear that she was very surprised from all her words and gestures.

I was someone who had no intention of getting married but now I had changed my mind I said slowly: "No, you don't know her.

I just met her I don't know her family either my mother snobbish looked at me and said: forget her and just move on I will introduce you a good girl …..

I said seriously: But I love her I want her my mother said in a kind tone: my dear I didn't understand when you fell in love I was embrassed she said again: you know your father's morals If that girl isn't at our level he will not accept I knew my father well, he was very strict we had to give a reason for everything even to breath.

For example: why are you breathing fast?!

Or why are you breathing slowly?!

In our house, my father always had the last word I don't know if it was because of love or coercion, but I never remember my mother disagreeing with him.

I was like that submissive and calm I don't remember disagreeing with my father I loved my father as much as the whole world, but he was strict towards us I don't know what kind of reward he was going to get from the world that paid it so mush the life of my mother and I and all our moments.

Were based on my father's wishes and dislikes but in the case of Nahid the case was different love made me brave I fought for my love I stood in front of my father who was the dearest person in my life but what I wanted didn't happen…..sir, what are you doing? You are here since morning!

She said again: what is it?! ………why are you looking?

Are you having a fight?

I hate the way girls talk like this I said something to her under my breath what………what……what did you say?? ……

I remember they day Nahid got into my car and said: "everyone knows rich people in the same street where you have a car exhibition with expensive cars I rented a shop under the stairs and I worked there I searched all the shops under the stairs of that street but Nahid wasn't there: there was only one shop that its door was closed.

She must work here that girl sat again: hey man! I was with you!

What did you say?……. I was about to answer when a soft and gentle female voice said: hello Mr. Fardin are you ok? She was beautiful and kind her face and voice was attractive for me but I didn't know her!

Breath Hold

I said under my breath: hello …..Thank you It was if she was familiar with that one girl she introduced me to her didn't you know the man? "Farhad car exhibition" on the same street ..it's very big….. it belongs to this gentleman. She was praising so much that I thought "Iran" belonged to me the girl widened her eyes in surprise. The discolored lens in her eyes remind me of wild cats she opened and closed her red prosthetic lips and said: oh,……..

I'm sorry…….why didn't you introduce yourself earlier? I smirked and said: you have time to Introduced myself she lowered her voice and flirtatiously said: you have been here since morning I thought you were idle people.

That one lady said: can I help you?

I didn't want them to think about me I thought to myself and pointed to the closed door of the shop and said: I have a word with the owner of this shop.

She asked with surprise: with it's owner?

I quickly changed my words and said: I have a word with someone who works here, not with the owner that coquetted girl said: Nahid used to do nail extentions here when I heard Nahid's name, I got confused and said: yes……yes, she is herself I have a word with Nahid they both looked at each other is surprise the coquetted girl raised her eye brows and said: does she owe you…….? I mean did she borrow money from you?

I didn't like her inappropriate question I frowned and said: It's a personal matter "I mean, It's none of your business ……"she shrugged her shoulders and said: "she has not come for two weeks" I asked: Do you have her number phone or address?

Breath Hold

Dear Madam .... I have a duty to do with Nahid I have to see her that one lady told: Fariba..... he is a respectable gentleman if you have Nahid's numbers, give it to him my face was begging.

I was shaking I was trying not to let them understand but they understood shehat closed her eyes and said: what are you doing with her?....... how lucky is this girl .....!

It was clear that she is jealous......... in order to reduce her jealousy and to get the address, I said: her cheque has bounced.

She said: that girl is a swindler so that's why her shop is closed she told me again your money and cheque will not be returned because Nahid and her family have no money.

She stared at me and said: cash the cheque and put her in the jail I thought to myself a little and paused and said:

yes ..... I have the same intention but I don't have her address she was happy like an evil and said: well, you would have said earlier why you wanted her address just don't tell her that you got it from me sure..... I had strange feeling I felt both close to him and far away! I felt she was inside me she had became a part of me. My heart my brain and my mind became Nahid. Nahid ....Nahid ....

It was a strange feeling I love it a mind feeling of longing and sadness a mind feeling of madness. " love is a hunt that even if your narrow goes wrong its pleasure will remain in the corner of your heart for ever........

In the corner of the prison, I enjoyed by reviewing my love memories.

I walked alone in the prison yard suddenly a scream was heard from the corridor it was the sound of beating with a baton a prisoner, a soldier and a prison guard came to the yard. A can of castor oil was in the guard's hand, and while cursing the prisoner he shouted: "If you don't eat this I will crush you with a baton".

I don't eat, I feel sick and stomach cramp again the guard cursed him and beat him with a baton then they tide him to a iron pole in the yard and forced him to eat 2 bottles of castor oil. His bowels had to be emptied because he was suspected of carrying several packeg 's of drugs that he had swallowed they went and closed the door of yard it's like they didn't understand that I was there.

I wanted to go back inside but the door was locked I had to stay there until the guard came back I sat on the platform in the corner of the yard I leaned my head against the rough wall. High walls and barbed wire made me feel bad I took a few deep breathes, but I felt that there was no air even in the yard.

Breath Hold

I was day time but the sky was black! Like my heart like the hearts of all prisoners the sky of inside the prison is diffent from the sky of outside very much …… there was a noise that pulled me out of my thoughts the prisoner had passed out those 2 packages of drugs with his feces he began to swallow them again his feces were smeared on his head and face suddenly they hit him on the head and face with batons his whole body was coverd in blood and feces this time he vomited the packages with blood seeing this sence made me feel bad this is the last station of the world humanity …..!!

What does in mean…….??

It has no meaning for me it is less as long as we are outside and are free and live comfortably, we think that we are human. But here at the end of the world I understood what human means!

The most wild and predatory creature is the human being in prison I leaned against the wall I had a headache I wanted to bang my head against the wall what happened Farhad …..?

You are very sad …. It was Mikaeil ……… he and his voice gave me peace who said Baha'is are impure!!!!? if there was a human being in that hell he was only Mikaeil.

He sat next to me and gave me a cigarette I put my head on his knees and cried he said with tears: what happened, brother?

As if I was speech less, I said in a very low voice: pray that they will execute me soon I can't stand it anymore he caressed my hair with his hand and said: don't say that, my dear you are a man , increase your tolerance and be strong …..?! How …….?! I smoked a few cigarettes and calm down I wanted to see my doughter " Asl" I felt that I had forgotten his face I wanted to hug her tightly Mikaeil was still sitting next to me we were both silent the sound of someone crying came from inside the prison I looked to wards the sound I asked Mikaeil: who is he? He just entered the prison.

Why is he crying? It was as if Mikaeil wanted to cry, but he controlled himself this made me sad more and I said: Is something wrong? That child is only 19 years old who?! The one who is crying? He nodded his head and said: yes……. Last night, two night shift guards raped him in solitary confinement he is very upset It was as if I was speechless my tears flowed silently Mikaeil was also crying " God" I have a bone to pick with you …….

I' m sad ….God…….. why so much cruelty …….. why so much oppression………

The sun hits my head. The weather was very hot It was a small house and was the address again and put my hand on the bell, put I didn't ring.

What to say? Tell them who am I? …….. And who have I come to? What should I say if her brother or her father comes to the door?

I stood a side and stared at the door everyone who passed by me looked at me and I was embarrassed I moved a little away from their house I was hoping that she would come to the door herself the door of the house opened a man with a thick mustache came out I took my mobile phone and pretended to be busy when he passed by me, I felt that he was looking at me so, he has a brother I had a bad feeling his face was like criminals or maybe I thought so, because of his mustache.

The heat of the sun bothered me a little further there was a lamp post willow branches hung from the walls of a old house I stood under its shadow, next to the lamp post Its better now.

I stood with one foot on the wall and one on the floor staring at their door.

Breath Hold

It was 4-5 in the afternoon the sun shines non-stop It was the middle of summer It was very hot I put a cigarette in the corner of my mouth and lit it I was stressed once, I saw a shadow he took the collar of my shirt in his hand suddenly he slapped me and I almost fell to the ground he shouted: who are you waiting for?

With in the seconds, I was surrounded by people they all had mustaches some of them were women each of them said something…….well done ….. you beat him well there is no one like you a woman who was wearing a flowery veil said: Yes…….I have been looking at him from the window for an hour he doesn't look like a thief . Another man with a mustache said he deceives and abduct women I remembered what my father said:

" always avoid those who have a lot of prejudice, but have little understanding and literacy "these are dangerous people who kill people out of ignorance and prejudice and are proud fit.

They didn't even let me explain they surrounded me and condemned me in such a way that I thought I did something really bad once I heard a pleasant voice:

Hello ……..MrFardin……..!! What are you doing here?! Half of the crowd turned towards the sound and the other half stared at me one of those mustachioed men who also had thick mustaches said in a hoarse voice: Nahid, do you know this man? Nahid said: he is Mr.Fardin the Fardin car exhibition on jomhour street is for him.

As if all the problems were solved with this word! They didn't even apologize and left Nahid was still looking surprised, but it was clear from her eyes that she was happy I was no longer stressed I had found my lost one nothing mattered to me anymore what are you doing here Mr.Fardin?!

I stared at her I just looked at her for a moment I loved her very much there was a special and beautiful sadness in my voice.

Breath Hold

I said: don't you know why I' am here?! No, I don't know.......! I said
firmly: I loved you! She just looked at me with surprise I said: word by
word of your not's have filled all my moments she cried this was the most
beautiful tear I had ever seen In one of her not's , she wrote :" I love you,
my Farhad, forever". I looked into her eyes and said: I want you forever
she was laughing and crying at the same time.

Chapter: 7

It was the middle of the night Monday night were different these nights were called "cleansing" for us the prisoners, it was as if we were dying and coming back to life every second behind of our cell was a small yard that was reversed for executed people they called it:

"Yard of the dead"

On Mondays, before sunshine usually 3 or 4 people would come to this yard we didn't see them, but their voice was painful for us. I had ague I wrapped the blanket around myself I was still sleeping on the prison floor hearing the prisoner's voice hit my head like a hammer.

Breath Hold

I swear to God …… have mercy on me ……...I just turned 20 years old
………..

His voice was shaking and he was crying at the moment of execution, the voices of executed were different from the voices of all the people in the world.

There was something special in their voice that one would explode from the inside when hearing it thing like:

Sadness ……...hatred……...shouting………death……. and begging…….begging were many in their voices.

A prisoner's voice was raised he was begging and crying I swear to God I' m innocent what did I say?!

I just said that our salary is low…….

I said that you didn't pay our salary for 5 months I was completely wrong I don't want salary just set me free the sounds stopped moments later the bodies were hanged……...

Once I seemed to go into a trance there were ropes and stools as far as the eye could see. Thousands of ropes was My head was above all those ropes the knot of the ropes was pressing under my troat My body was loose and hanging I pushed thr tools on by one I was laughing out loud and madly.

"Wisdom and madness"!!!!!!!! you can't draw a line between them these two are together madness is in the middle of the brain like" crying and laughing" or "Night and Day " Farhad?.........Farhad?........ What happened to you? Are you shaking?......

Mikaeil was on top of me and shaking me I opened my eyes.........I half-deadly said: I was executed....... I was relieved.

Mikaeil wiped the corner of my lips with his hand and said:

His mouth is foaming he threw his blanket on me you are shivering.......

You are cold.

I crie...........

Mikaeil said:

Breath Hold

Boys don't cry.

But he was also crying.

I understood from the tone of his voice.

" To tell the truth..........! Even before prison whenever I was sad I used to cry in my lone lines. Her in prison if we don't cry we will die".

What happened Farhad?! I can't see your tears.

I was surprised I didn't understand when he entered before I wiped my tears I felt his warm fingers on my face he dried my face my father's voice was still coming listen.........!

I will not allow you to marry into that worthless and law-class family.

I got angry once and went out of my room and stood in front of my father while my voice. Was shaking I said: that girl isn't worthless, just that her financial level is lower than ours. My father raised his voice and said:

My son be wise and don't pay. Attention to what your heart says don't value your heart so much. The heart makes excuses you should not give it ever thing it wants some people or something are more beautiful when they are faraway but when they are close, you see that they are nothing my son don't be fooled make a decision with your mind and marry with a girl who can be a good mother for your child I lowered my head and said slowly:

How do you know that Nahid doesn't has these characteristics??

He took a bunch of his hair in his fist and advised me:

"I wasn't born yesterday" I have experience I know people much better than you why do you think I'm so short-sightedness that I oppose them because of their financial situation?

I researched about them her family remains like a "marsh" Nahid is a flower in the marsh my son accept that "family" is like the root of a person the root of this girl is rotten.

Breath Hold

My father didn't know it was too late the damage was done my heart had its decision I didn't dare raise my voice to my father I was totally embarrassed. But I said my word:

I love Nahid whoever she is and I left the house I make decisions with my heart and don't pay attention to my wisdom how many times does a person fall in love in his whole life? If there is no love I don't want that life? and I don't want children either what does life even mean?! You marry with someone who is just a "woman"? Or good mother to your child?..... You work all day for that?! No, I hate this kind of life I also hate my mother's relationship with my father.

Yes, sir…….sure…….whatever you say, sir…..so what about her……?! Why doesn't my dad obey my mom for once? My mom doesn't have feelings?!........ I hate this "patriarchy" life" I hated myself too, because I just obeyed. I want to not be like this anymore.

I want my wife to be happy and sometimes disobedient sometimes she say's "No" to me and disagrees with me sometimes we fight and yell at each other I hate weake women I don't like women who only talk about their pains and sorrows their crises and words in privet I want a life partner and companion.

I want someone who will tell me all her pains and sorrows, their cries and laughs, not in her solitude many times I saw my mother crying alone and talking to herself. I always say to myself: where is my father in my mother's loving heart? My father isn't a bad person and I have never met anyone more kind than him but they didn't understand the meaning of life or maybe I don't like this kind of life this type of life is specific to their generation our generation is different this generation doesn't want a quiet women, it wants a women full of energy, full of love words, and full of colored roses the world of our generation is colorful and crowded but the world of our parent's generation is black and white, silent and fragrant sometimes I hate this silence and peace.

Breath Hold

But, "you have your head in the clouds". When Nahid's hand were in my hand's it was as if the world was in my hands my heart was full of love and hope her hands were my whole world I pressed harder ....sudden I felt that my hand was empty I opened my hand and looked, it was empty........ Where are you Nahid?! Were are your hands?........ Now, I need your hands here........I'm shaking , Nahid!!!!

Mikaeil wrapped the blanket around me tighter and said:

What's up boy?! .... Calm down........ What are you doing with yourself?! I loved his voice so much it gave me peace he gave me a cigarette...... a cigarette is heaven for a prisoner. .... Many times, when the executioners are brought to the execution, and asked for their last wish, they only ask for a cigarette they smoke a cigarette and then it's over sometimes, I say to myself: this is the end of all dreams!

A cigarette .... damn this world curse here that the last wish of a person is a cigarette that's when you wish for hell I'm sure hell is better than here at least smoke and fire aren't the last wish of a person.

Chapter: 8

A new prisoner had entered the prison he doesn't talk to anyone he was old and had a familiar face I'm sure I've been him outside the prison before where had I seen him……?!

I wasn't a curious person but I don't know why I wanted to know more about him Ruaof………? Yes…… what is it bro?

Breath Hold

I asked him slowly:

What do you know about this new prisoner (while pointing at him)?

Raouf was known as BBC among the prisoners he knew everything and everyone. He was a teacher and he was in prison for ten years his sentence was life imprisonment and he was really kind like his name while narrowing his eyes and looking at me, he said: why is it important to you?!

His face is familiar to me. As you can see he doesn't talk to anyone but as far as I know, he was making and selling drugs.

They say that his death sentence has been issued I heard that when the judge read his death sentence in the court he said loudly to him: "I will bury you under a lot of money and come out……."

I asked in surprise :

Really?!

Raouf mockingly said:

It's just for money a lot of death sentences came here but they were released in less than two weeks.

I became hopeful and asked happily and unbelievably:

Are you right?!

Raouf sighed heartly and said:

You have a long way to find out where this is!! Here, innocent people are imprisoned, then hanged real sinners don't come here if they come, they are here temporarily and they are quickly released and go out does that mean.

I can be free?

I don't want you to be disappointed, but God's miracle can save us because you and I are political prisoners and there is the end of the world for us I went to the new comer man and sat next to him.

Hello ……..

He didn't answer me.

I'm itatingly some prisoners, I said: well come to our prison cell he said with his deep voice: "you don't need to say welcome to come here, "colored chicken"

Do you think there is your father's hotel?!

Breath Hold

It was clear that he had information about me. Because of the honey color of my eyes and the color of my hair, which was almost light, some of my friends called me "color chick" your face is very familiar to me…..

But I don't remember where I saw you?! He looked at me and said:

"You are the son-in-law of Sadegh (RIP)…… suddenly my breath was trapped in my chest…….I couldn't breath I tried so hard but I couldn't my face was bruised the knot of the rope is pressing on my throat the chair had fallen under my feet and my feet couldn't reach the ground I could not scream I was just shaking my hands and feet in the air they say: "cowards die many times before their death."

I say it is thousand times worse and scarier than death. Death takes a person life once and get rid of it but "fear of dying" takes a person's life moment and second by second many people commit suicide in prison to get out sooner.

Because the thought of dying is terrible no one can understand this except an executioner there were drops of water on my face I opened my eyes my friends were on top of me.

I looked at the newly arrived prisoner I had many question I wanted to know more from all my family especially Nahid and my daughter.

He must have had information about them he was also looking at me while playing with his mustache he opened his eyes and said:

You didn't know?!......... No one comes to see you?!

I still couldn't breath properly.

Mikaeil said for me:

He is for bidden to visit he played with his mustache again and cautiously said:

Well…….. They executed sadegh a few months ago…. So they finally executed him ….. Tears rolled down my eyes, not for sadegh but more for myself I could be executed………

For whom?!..... For what?! For someone who was finaly executed I was sacrificed…… and this caused me more torment than anything else.

Breath Hold

It was time to go to the prison yard I went to the yard I wanted to cry..........

Chapter: 9

The arguments between me and my father had started I insisted:

Only Nahid ……….Nahid……Nahid.

Farhad…….Farhad, where are you boy?!

It was my father's voice he was sitting on the sofa his face turned red and he was very angry he pointed to sit down.

Breath Hold

I sat in front of him my mom was stressed she looked at me pleadingly now that I remember I feel very sorry for her she said to my father:

Sir, can I bring you some tea?

No, nothing goes down my throat.

I didn't understand their frustration at that time I didn't understand why I had become so bold look, son I want to talk you logically he tried not to speak loudly, but he was not very Successful.

Yes…… I want to introduce each and every member of Nahid's family to you I will start with his father first:

He is an unemployed person who is taking drugs from morning till night.

I said under my breath: well, what does it have to do with me?!

My father pretended that he didn't hear me, but hi did he became angrier but controlled himself my mom motioned to me from the kitchen to say nothing.

He said again:

But her brother…… her brother's name is Babak he was in prison for several months, but I don't know what and why …..! It's not really important he has a criminal record they say he used to use drugs but now he doesn't use them anymore I said again under my breath:

Thank God he doesn't use it anymore.

Breath Hold

My father's surprise increased he couldn't believe that I would sit in front of him and talk like this before when my father spoke we just obeyed.

But now I didn't obey him I wanted to say "no…..no……no" to all my father's words, I wanted to break the rules my father stared at me he just looked at me for a few moments in silence sudden, said in a louder voice than before:

Do you know Nahid's older sister is married to a blind man?!

Well…… is it a crime to marry a blind person?! This time he shouted: the reason is important, son!

Why should a young girl marry a blind old man? I said slowly:

Dad …….we should not enter into the private lives of others.

I don't think this matter is related.

To us he suddenly shouted:

"It's relevant ….."

I shuddered from the loudness of his voice and immediately became silent I peeked at my mother she was shaking and her look was still pleading my heart burned for my mother even for my father I didn't like to see him in that state.

I felt bad for myself because of my selfishness I used to upset them.

But I loved Nahid, I loved her who should I tell?!

How can I tell them to understand and be satisfied? I wanted to shout like my father and say that I love Nahid.

My father continued: they say her sister wasn't a good girl do you know what it means …….? It means that she was a prostitute!!

Breath Hold

For this reason, she had to marry a blind man

I got up angrily I wanted to shout like my father but I didn't allow myself to do so I just said: "I don't care".

My father shouted again:

It must be important to you!

It must be important to you that they say her sister is a prostitute I am a honorable man understand, boy……. Understand…….!

His voice was so loud that it shook the windows!

I looked at my mother she was crying I was crying too. I came out of the house latar I asked Noushin herself I didn't accept my father's words. But I also wondered why Noushin married an elderly blind man!!!

I had justified myself that they had fallen in love but I knew very well that my words were irrational Is it possible for a beautiful and young girl to fall in love with a blind and old man?! "We humans sometimes deceive ourselves to justify ourselves we lie to ourselves to be believe and this is a stupid thing but sometimes you need to be stupid to get what you want Nashin?

Can I ask you a personal question?

Her beautiful face was sad……. She didn't say anything I wanted ask why she married to said: but I didn't say I think it's very unfair to ask her why, you married a blind man instead I asked: why do you always wear black?

I have never seen you wear colored clothes! She said: I relay like to have a red bag and shoes I really want a red or yellow coat.

Breath Hold

I love colorful scarves do you think I don't like to wear colorful clothes? I was tired of wearing dark clothes I asked her surprisedly:

well, who doesn't let you wear colored clothes?

Tears gathered in her eyes and she said: people's look and their mental illness she paused a it and said: if I wear a red coat all looks will turn to me again why again?!

Has something like this happened before?!

I know you have heard a lot of about me but I swear to God what they say about me is not true here our town is very small. Everyone will understand if any one does a small thing for example if you drink water everyone will understand I wish they only say that he drank water but they say: he drank alcohol!!! If you take a simple pill, they call you an addict.

Addicted to psychedelic pills!

I couldn't accept her words. I thought she was justifying her actions and behaviors does that mean they are hostile to you?

She bit her lip and thought…..

A little later she said: Nader and I were friends we loved each other too much ……at least I thought so……. We were going to get married I was only 18 years old a small mistake made people say these things about me. The words that are still going on…..Nader invited me to go to his house no one was there….

(She started crying) we were drinking tea. But it didn't taste good that tea was the best tea of my life because Nader made it for me. He told a joke that was not funny at all but I laughed with all my heart as he Laughed too they knocked on the door and Nader opened it.

It was police! They took us out of the house in the worst condition one of the neighbors informed the police that there are prostitutes in this house this incident made people say irrelevant things about me they called me" bitch" and "notorious" they said so much that even Nader believed that I was a promiscuous…….. And he refused to marry me.

Breath Hold

Being "prejudice" and "ignorance" together can form a strong team, so they can destroy "love" …….

I was ashamed of my family I had made them dishonorable my brother "Babak" used to beat me whenever he was angry I was not upset, but my heart was burning to myself what had.

I done?

Is it a crime to love?

Is falling in love a crime?

Is it a crime to trust someone?

I trusted Nader and went to his house that's all …..I swear to God that nothing happened between us.

I don't know for what sin I was punished like this. She said her last sentences with tears………

She put her hands on her face cried when she calmed down a bit she said: I met said at the Sametime.

His financial situation was good he worked in the "home for the orphans" and was their teacher and he was 15 years older than me.

One day I said:

To him why don't you get married?

He said: who will marry with me?

Maybe I can marry someone like myself ……she paused and said bitterly:

I told him will you marry me!!

The poor man was shocked he said:

Are you kidding me?

My eyes filled with tears ….the only good thing was that he couldn't see…. I laughed forcibly so that he could hear my laughter. Laughing at the top of misery. They say that those who commit suicide, smile at the last moment. Now I understand the meaning of their laughing a smile mixed with "Poison" I said: I'm serious.

I want to marry you?

Breath Hold

Saied said:

I would like to know the reason.

I'm sure it's not love.

I said angrily:

Damn love ……..who said the marriage should be based on love ask
me……. Marriage should be based on reason it should be on the basis that
people are suitable for each other in every way……. I say that we are
suitable for marriage you have money and I have no money you are blind
and I can see so we can complete each other that's enough ……It's enough
that we have a house and live toghether, love and feelings are not very
important I married Saied in less than a week 2 and went to his house no
one said anything bad about me.

Bad looks were gone most importantly I was no longer with my family
every day and I was less embarrassed even widows don't get married like
me, but I got marrid like this.

Chapter: 10

I was looking at that man with a thick mustache he was smoking I sat next to his bed he looked at me but said nothing I said with difficulty:

I don't know from outside from my family from my wife and child, from Babak …….. He touched his mustache and said:

At that time, when you were just arrested and your news was all over the place they said in the town that you father came and took Nahid and your daughter with himself because there was no one to take care of them.

Breath Hold

They executed sadeq at the same time Babak was also sentenced to life imprisonment for complicity with you their mother also suffered a stroke after the execution of sadeq and became paralyzed and lives with her daughter Noshin.

I felt like a person who is lying in a grave and every moment a little dirt is poured on him I could feel small particles of dirt in my throat I felt relieved about my wife and my child because my father was with them he offered.

Me a cigarette I took one and put it on the corner of my lips he fired it for me.

He didn't seem like a bad person he said in his deep voice: I'm sure none of you understood how these things happened to you! I didn't understand what he meant and I looked at him confusedly I asked what does that mean?!

He looked at me with contempt and said:

"Don't you understand?!

I mean, you don't understand who is your enemy.

You didn't understand who put drugs in your car.

I jumped up and asked angrily:

Who?!! Who did this!!!

He said calmly: "sit down, kid!" if I had done that, I would not have told you so who did this?! Do you know Mehrdad?

Yes……he was Babak's close friend………..yes…….!

He had placed it in the car! I was very surprised I couldn't believe it!!!!

I asked : why ?!!! For what?!!

He said calmly: It's better not to know! If you find out the reason, you will be harassed in prison I insisted:

Breath Hold

I need to know why he did this??

His shrugged his shoulders and said:

Mehrdad was in love with Nahid for several years but Nahid didn't accept. Mehrdad's job was to distribute of drugs and crack he was in prison when you came otherwise, he wouldn't let you get married he is a villain when he was released, you were married and had a child. But Mehrdad didn't give up he worked for me he was always plotting for Nahid one day before sadeq's arrest, he said to Nahid : Divorce your has band, otherwise I will not let you live easily Nahid also told him: Farhad is much more valuable to me than you and I will never divorce him the imprisoned man played with his mustache again and said:

Nahid had said something bad and had made Mehrdad very angry that night you were guest at sadiq's house and your car was parked outside the house Mehrdad put 2 kilos of drugs in the car.

He thought that the police would arrest you, but he didn't know that sadiq was going to get into the car tomorrow he reported the number and details of the car to the police later we found out that sadiq was arrested and the poor man was executed while he was innocent.

As he was playing with his mustache, the man said:

Son! Sadiq's family was not at your level It is a pity that you married this girl what did Nahid have that you fell in love with?!

I was on the verge of tears my father's words kept repeating in my head:" her family is like a swamp …..Aswamp …….Nahid is flower in a swamp …….family is the root of a person, understand! ………the root of this girl is rotten……. I found out too late when I realized that every moment I was getting closer to the time of execution.

Breath Hold

Chapter: 11

It was morning the door of the cell opened to go prison yard.

The guard looked at me he pointed at me with his hand and said:

You….Farhad Fardin.

Go to the ward chief's room, Mr. Bahrami.

I felt my blood freeze I didn't know what does he want to see me?!

I felt Mikaeil's warm and kind and on my shoulder don't be afraid …..God wiling its nothing slowly so that only Mikaeil could hear I said:

Mikaeil…..I' m afraid Bahrami is a scoun drelly man I'm afraid of his eyes.

Mikaeil was silent he had nothing to say.

I knew, I had to go ……..Mikaeil came with me halfway a the and of the corridor, the guard didn't allow him to come I reached the door of Bahrami's room and knocked a few times my hands were shaking……..

Come on……..

His voice was scary.

I entered the room his eyes were like the eyes of a toad and he had an ugly face his eye brows were also half his head was bald and it sparkled under the light of the lamp he pointed to the chair and said:

Sit…….

I sat I swallowed hard.

He poured me a glass of rotgut/ hooch and put it on the table he said:

"Eat young man……eat to be happy ……I was silent because of fear "

I coughed and said:

Breath Hold

He shouted and said:

These words are for outside of this room ……for outside of the prison….
Her I will tell you what you are or are not you got it??

Then he laughed his laugh was also ugly he had drunk himself when he
talks he smell I took the glass My hand was shaking I held it tighter I
could not stop my hand shaking I drank a few sips he said:

Eat more I ate again I ate until the end I was nauseous I wanted to vomit
after a while I felt good he gave me 2 packs of cigarettes and said:

It's for you It was giving me heaven I said in my heart: what a good man
he is , I was afraid of him or nothing sudden he said: damn you! Why are
you so beautiful? Can a boy be so hand some!!!

It was clear from his voice and movements that he had drunk a lot sudden, he came closer to me and said: you are beautiful and that makes me want to spend a night with you.

I pushed him back and said: hey idiot what are you doing?!!

Suddenly, he got angry and laughed loudly with a movement, he took the carpet blade and put it under my throat he said slowly:

No one can hear you........so shut up and let me do it I was able to tame people like you what would happen if I didn't listen to him?!

He said softly in my ear: you have amazing eyes......you made me fall in love with you........the feeling of his warm breath on my face made me feel very bad when his mouth opened the smell of hooch came out I was crying my tears were sitting on my face one after another.

Breath Hold

I felt humiliated I wanted to hang myself ……. I pulled the blanket over my head in the cell "Father, do you remember how sensitive you were about me, that being home at night?

When it was getting dark, you would get angry if I was outside you said: It doesn't matter for a girl or a boy….. Staying out at night makes a person be prostitute.

"Father, you aren't here to see me became a prostitute I hope you will never understand what happened to me….. I heard.

Mikaeil's voice: what happened to you, Farhad? What did Bahrami do with you?

I was crying and couldn't answer I barely said a few words: leave me alone …..Mikaeil.

I was lying on the floor and I was very sad about what happened.

To me….."Nahid, look at my hand, its shaking I feel like this whenever you are by my side there is a commotion in my heart then they tell me to make a decision with your mind do you think so? Why should the mind decide for the heart?

We both laughed out loud…..

Nahid?

Yes my dear …..When you are not by my side my heart is restless.

Farhad, I'm afraid from what…..?

I'm with you I'm afraid that one day you will not love me I held her hair in my hand and said: I'm addicted to the fragrance of your hair. How can I not love you? Memories are always with people in the worst condition. You feel that you have no feeling for them It's seems ridiculous even to you but they are always in your mind to remind you how stupid you were……..!

I don't know have you ever felt server pain due to sadness? I had …..

Breath Hold

I had 2 packs of cigarettes I smoked them all quickly Mikaeil was leaning on the iron bars I saw that he was looking at me he said:

Did you find a treasure?

His meant was cigarettes he said again: don't smoke too much because of your lungs I didn't feel like answering it. I smirked at him in my heart and said:

"These lungs are going to go underground soon".

It was night but it was not time of sleep yet the door of the cell opened and two young men pushed in every one's voice was raised there isn't enough space…. Take them to another cell….

Half of us sleep on the floor …….

There is also not enough space on the floor …….some of them grumbled under their breath, but everyone knew that their protest was useless.

The guard closed the iron door and said: two of you will be executed tomorrow.

Everyone was silent and thought in his mind that I will be executed tomorrow I wanted to kill that guard so that he doesn't get on our nerves like this we spent all our moments in despair and wating until seconds minutes hours days and night passed……. But these moments passed very slowly sometimes it didn't pass at all.

" Nahid you didn't see me in my deadly moments and you will not see me later these moment of suffering and humiliation only happened to me because of my love for you damn my lover's heart…..!

My dear father ….never forgive me may be not forgiving me, my emotional distress will be reduced I wish I would have listened to you those days when you shouted and advised me my dear father, you don't know what hard times I spend here.

Nahid maybe neither you nor your family were bad but we weren't suitable for marriage and now I will hardly pay for this mistake.

Breath Hold

Now I understand the meaning of: "Birds of a feather flock together. " Because in this way someone like me is sacrificed I sacrificed, Nahid.

Mikaeil and Raouf were on top of the two newly arrived prisoners all their bodies were bloody the marks of the whip were all over their bodies they were two brothers their names were Hamza and Jafar they were from Ahvaz. One of them was very young Hamza was abut 18 years old and Jafar was abut 23 year old all of Hamza's front teeth were broken his lip was torn near his chin his eyes were bruised and bloody Jafar couldn't move much his legs were broken one of his arms was broken from the shoulder the marks of the whip was on his face …… we were used to seeing such things I couldn't bear to see blood before but now I'm used to it in the morning the cell door opened.

It was time to go to the yard……

The guard said to the man with the mustache, who mustache who was a friend of sadiq, (my father- in- low) " pack your things you're free".

The other looked at him with regret he was only in prison for 3 days!

While he should have been executed but he was released ….! It was very similar to the "mafia" game….!

That man touched his mustache and said: they brought me here by mistake I said that, I 'm only here for 2-3 days.

Then the guard pointed to two of the prisoners: Esmaeil Mahmoudi, shahram soleymani, go to back of the cell.

No one looked at them.

I came out of my cell those who went behind the cell, should have been executed I didn't want to talk to anyone at all I went and sat in the corner of the yard.

Raouf came and sat next to me what happened to you?!

Why are you upset for a few days?!

My throat hurt when I spoke I put my hand on my throat, pressed it and said:

Bahrami….. He is a very mean person…..he said: I know ……I heard a lot about him.

Breath Hold

I looked at Raouf's face and said: in your opinion we can't do anything…..?

Raouf looked at the high walls of the prison and said:

"Outside the prison the voice of our demand for our rights didn't reach anywhere" here with these high walls our, voices can't be heard at all.

Raouf, why are you here? Why were you sentenced to life imprisonment?!

He said sadly: I always thought that prison is a place for murderers and criminals I was so stupid prisons are built for people like us who be silent and can't take our rights from them…..have you ever been unable to buy a loaf of bread?!

It's very hard and painful when you child is hungry but doesn't protest……. He paused a bit and controlled his crying and said:

Sometimes I saw that my child was only eating a piece of bread I just looked at him, like a foal, but I couldn't do anything why didn't they pay our salaries?! In a country like Iran, which is rich in every aspect it's people don't live in prosperity these things are the pain and sorrow for a nation……..

My child's leg was broken, I had no money to take him to the doctor I tied his leg with two wooden boards and a piece of cloth It had been about 7-8 months that they hadn't pay my salary and the rest of the teachers in the village they said that the ministry of education has no bud get!!! When I protested, they brought me here for what crime????

"For the crime acting against national security" …….!

He laughed out of anger and said:

It's funny ……isn't it?! I said:

Nothing is done properly in our country I am sure that the law of the forest is better than the law of our country, because its ruler is the lions of the forest.

Breath Hold

Chapter: 12

My pillow was hard as a rock, I put it side and crumpled my blanket, and put it under my head the sound of the two executioners scream and cries clearly came from the back of the cell I feel cold I took the blanket again and put it on myself I put my hands on my ears so that I don't hear them.

My father's voice echoed in my ears my son, this girl isn't suitable for marriage I promise you, if you want another girl, I won't say anything I was reckless and said: I only want Nahid.

My father stared into my eyes he didn't believe all this recklessness he was very angry and he said: I will deprive you of your in heritance……

I slowly said: it doesn't matter.

He put his hand on his heart, took a deep breath and said:

Tell them that we are going to propose to their daughter this weekend I came very happy I didn't think he would accept it so soon I wanted to jump into his arms and scream for joy I looked at my mom, she was looking at me with a smile.

A smile with sadness ….. I didn't understand many things at that time, maybe I didn't want to understand ….I saw my father put his hand on his heart but I didn't pay attention only " love" was important to me I my mother's crying and smiling face, but only her smile was important to me….

"My tears, don't fall on my face tonight men just want a cigarette instead of crying "

My hands were in Nahid's hands, I was excited like children.

Breath Hold

I happily said:

Nahid ……..you can't believe it…..finally, my father was satisfied.

Nahid screamed and laughed with happiness.

Farhad………..I feel that the world is in my hands.

I looked at her hands she held hand tightly.

I was saying to myself:

Our hands will remain like this forever and will not open I wish that when we make decisions with our hearts we used our intellect a little.

Nahid……… did you know that if love is too much, it turns into madness?

Nahid smiled and said: do you mean to say that you have gone insane?

We were in the car I wrapped my hand around her neck and said: I love this madness.

Nahid "on the planet, you are the best creature for me.

I hugged her tighter and read out loud a sentence from her notebook: "
Your eyes have changed my life…….." she laughed and said:

Don't you want to return my notebook?

"I firmly said:

Never………..never……

When I sleep at night I put your not book on my heart.

Nahid was looking at me with love and saying under his breath:

I love you Farhad ……

Forever ………

Forever……….

Forever……..

I put my hands in my ears so I don't hear this damn sentence I felt bad.

Breath Hold

I heart this sentence every day and every moment in prison I hate this sentence

Forever........

Forever......

Forever ....

I sat next to Hamza my heart was burning for him he was very young and had an innocent face he should have gone to nigh school and sat behind the school benches, but now he was behind bars.

I offered him a cigarette ......

No, I'm not a smoker.

He had big eyes and his face was burnt by the sun and turned brown half of his teeth were broken I said:

How old are you Hamza?.....

I will be seven teen soon you are very young......!

He said sadly:

Children in Ahvaz grow up quickly this is the nature of poverty people grow up fast I liked his voice and words I asked:

How old is your brother?

Jafar is 23 years old.

I knew they were political prisoners but I didn't know what their crime?

"I wasn't a curious person, but in prison one's sense of curiosity is activated …… In our cell, because everyone has either a death sentence or life imprisonment, no one spoke and was silent and waiting……. A deadly and indescribable.

Waiting……

Hamza looked at his brother, he was lying on the bed while he couldn't move at all …….he said:

"Our crime is action against national security, war with God and corruption on earth!

"I took a deep breath. Before I came to prison, if I under stood that some one's crime was " Warring God and corruption in the earth," I would have said: that he is a dangerous person and that he should be imprisoned tortured and executed but also those who are accused of these things are the most innocent people.

Breath Hold

" No matter how you say the truth, the answer is execution."

I don't know why I wanted to talk to him, but he didn't feel like talking " It was clear from his face that he wanted to cry, but I knew that if he talked, would calm down a bit, we the prisoners who were condemned to death, under stood each other well. I said:

What did you do……? Did you kill someone…..?

He put his hand on his throat and said: there is a lot of poverty and misery in Ahvaz our city is full of oil wells, but we don't asleep at night because of hunger we established a cultural institution we were all young in the institute we had about 20 active members maybe 40-50 people were inactive the name of our institution was " Al-Hawar".

There we held poetical content sessions at night we were talking about discrimination against Arab people and about people's poverty and how and from whom should get our rights at the sometime, several explosions took place in Ahvaz .

No one understood who the perpetrators of the explosion were….. We only know that it wasn't done by our group and our people who bombs in his own city?!

This bombing and explosion caused my friends to be chased and arrested all members of the group were arrested and subjected to the worst interrogations and torture to make them con fess to the bombing Its very hard to endure the interrogation and torture, very hard…….we were tortured in the worst way for several months in the secret detention center of Ahvaz ministry of "Intelligence" we confessed to everything they said, such as bombing, explosion, carrying out armed operations murders, and whatever else we could not think of but they said and we had to accept without any protest………. Twenty of us were sentenced to death and the rest to life imprisonment his tears wet his face you have to be very brave when you know you are going to be executed…..how can you breath how can you talk …….how you can spent the moments when you know you are going to die …….I'm sure if they were given a roap they would have hanged themselves in that moment I wish, time would go a little faster for us so that we would be executed sooner.

Breath Hold

It was lunch time and we had to go for lunch suddenly.

The cell door opened about 14 people entered with their helmets, batons, shields and pepper spray they threw tear gas and beat us with batons the sounds of moans and screams of the prisoners and the shouts of the guards filled the prison after a few minutes, they beat us and left we opened our eyes with difficulty ……..my friends were injured and bloody due to being beaten with a baton their legs and heads were broken the floor of the prison was coverd in blood.

The smell of blood torture threats bothered us my head was hurting and burning the baton had hit my head I barely put my hand on my wound to stop the bleeding but it was useless.

They had taken 4 people with them Hamza, Jafar, Asif and Tohid these 4 people were supposed to be executed in a few days later we found out that the execution of these people especially Hamza, who was very young had been covered by the media.

"Human Rights Organization" demanded the immediate cancellation of the execution of these 4 people but that night they executed all 4 of them they hadn't even delivered their bodies I had heard that after mass executions the bodies are buried in mass graves in an area called "Khavaran".

It doesn't matter if they hand over the bodies or not ……its better if they don't hand over the bodies because seeing the marks of torture on their bodies will hurt and upset their families.

Nahid you aren't know what it means of the when the morning comes and you are waiting for the names of the names of the executed people to be read?

You don't know what rape and humiliation mean?

Nahid it feels very bad to be humiliated by a man…….

Nahid, here you forget who are you…….

Breath Hold

You don't know whether you are a man.......a woman.........or a child?

Here you forget who are your parents ....even your name.

Nahid, you aren't here and you don't know what it means to see prison bars every day........sometimes.

I look at the bars so much, I feel like my whole body is pierced with them Do you know what is agnoy means? It is thousands of times worse than physical torture.

Nahid, I'm only 30 years old, but I feel like an old man who has lived for 1000 years. Nahid here it seems that time does not move forward and we are lost in time they say that a " woman" makes a man progress and reach him to the peak.

Nahid, you brought me to the peak of " humiliation"

Chapter: 13

We woke up in the morning with the noise of the guard I think it was winter and I was still sleeping on the floor of the cell the floor was very cold mosquitos were buzzing above us!

Can you find mosquitoes even in cold weather?! As if they were counting the moments for our execution we went to have breakfast my sense of touch and smell was gone the bread was hard as a rock and hard to swallow.

Breath Hold

But we were used to it in prison, everything becomes a habit for prisoners and these are painful for a prisoner.

We were in the yard when the guard approached me and said softly: go to Bahrami's room.

He has something to do with you I knew what he wanted to do I was used to it this habit was accompanied by humiliation tears and smoking……….

I sad on a chair in the room I was afraid of his eyes he said to me:

What's your name?

I said: I don't know………why did you come to prison?

I don't know ………what do you have to do with you?

I don't know ……..well done……..you listened well…….he came closer……his mouth smelled of rotgut ………….

Being imprisoned has a good effect on you It was clear that he was drunk while his hand was shaking he poured.

Me a drink in the glass I knew I had to eat at least when I was drinking it would be easier for me to bear all this humiliation I don't know if it was due to alcohol or something else, but Bahrami's body was shaking and his eyes were moving up and down he started praising under his breath:"

Those honey eyes of yours.......those beautiful eyes of yours...... hand's an boy.......

When he was done, he mastered on himself he stared at me I didn't want to look at him " Humiliation" had taken over my whole being like a monster I wanted to cut his head of with a knife then I would laugh out loud to get rid of this feeling he put two packs of cigarettes on the table he still talks like a drunk he said: well done ......always say "I don't know" you got it?

Breath Hold

I showed with my head movements that I understood my eyes were teary I didn't want a cigarette any more, I just wanted a rope.......

I was lying on the floor of the cell and looking at the ceiling here inside the walls and iron bars, "life" ids dead is there "life" outside these walls?

Farhad, what does life mean?

I don't understand you I mean, what are we born for.........?

What will happen?!..........what should we do.....?

The concept of life is meaning less to me.

She paused and said: you see, some people say we love life, I don't understand them. It was the middle of may we were in the middle of Damavand slopes.

It was wide plain and there was green everywhere as far as the eye could see I put my hand under my head and lay down and looked at the sky a gentle breeze blows I looked at Nahid.

The wind had thrown her scarf and her hair was dancing in the air this movement of her hair had fascinated me.

I said with a voice full of love and zeal:

Nahid, I love life

Nahid thought a little and said:

Well for you who are rich, it is like that you all love live why not be at all?!

The best house, the best car, the best clothes are for you. Life is yours as I was lying down, I turned to my side and put my hand under my head and said:

Nahid, do you know why we were born?

I mean you and me, not other people Nahid shrugged her shoulders and said indifferently: " You must say…….we were born to fall in love with each other" then she put her lips on her teeth and pressed.

Breath Hold

She said: how long do you think we are going to be in love? Two years….
There years ………five years…… what will happen in the end? Because
of these few years we have to live a life time?

I got up and couldn't believe that Nahid was saying these words! I said
angrily :

What does that mean ?!

Was that the love you were talking about?!

Was it only for 4-5 years?

She was surprised by my angry look and quickly repeated her words as
follows: Farhad, I didn't mean that be sure our love will last forever but
we don't feel like this in two or three years later we will lose our passion
and excitement this is the nature of love and people I was surprised who
did I fall in love with?!

Does Nahid fall in love with someone every day?!

But later I realized that Nahid was right " love is only" before marriage after marriage the excitement of" love" decreases Nahid had come to this conclusion earlier than me and I understood late do you know.

Why the love of "Shirin and Farhad" laili and Majnoun", " khosro and shirin" remained forever and wasn't erased from the minds?? Because they never married why did they have to get married?!

But at that time, I thought that if I don't marry Nahid I will surely die…..!!

I advised her firmly and said: Nahid, take care of your heart your heart shouldn't fall in love with someone every day…. I hate this kind of heart when will this winter end?

The floor of the cell is very cold I wrapped the blanket around myself and closed my eyes. The cell door opened with a sound every one woke up and looked at the door in the dark the guard entered in a dim light I rubbed my eyes more…. I could see right!! A half –naked woman……almost naked was with the guard!!

Breath Hold

The door opened and the woman entered…….the guard said:

"Evacuate bed number 3 quickly and hand over the new prisoner" then he closed the door and left the others were very surprised………what dosed that mean……….?!?

The woman slowly went to the bed the sound of our breath was complicated in the space everyone had heart beats Ali broke the silence and said:

Is this a new funny game?!

Mikaeil said: no, their intention is spiritual torture.

Abbass said: why do you say torture?

They sent us a nymph when they talked, their voices trembled their emotions their lust, All of their five senses which were silent in the prison were suddenly stirred up Raouf said:

"Be shamed, what are you talking about?"

Asghar said: please don't act like a teachers for us here.

In a jiffy, several people surrounded the woman.

Mikaeil said: friends……..whoever this woman is, she belongs to a family ……..please be careful sudden..

Abbass shouted:

Your words are like putting food in front of a hungry person……….anyone will eat. No one could stop them………ten people were surrounded by the woman's bed their chatter was coming from that woman.

she had a delicate voice that touches every man's heart they were right you couldn't stop thinking about her it's like they give you water in the desert and you don't drink is it possible?

All my attention was on the woman's voice I didn't understand what she was saying but her voice attracted me I was waiting for those few people to move away from the bed and go to her. Her voice was like two packs of cigarettes to me Saeed was lying next to me and I could hear his breathing and heart beat.

Breath Hold

I turned to him and said:

Is something wrong?! Why are you panting like that?

Farhad……when she talks, it's like I'm injected with morphine he held my hand tightly I said softly:

Are you ok?

His voice trembling ……..he said:

I seem to have over dosed…… Am I going to have a stroke?

I smiled mysteriously and said: I'm like you the voice of lust and emotions of guys and the woman's voice were mined together sometimes it was begging sometimes it was threats and force ……….no matter what I tried.

I couldn't sleep I wanted to go to her the boys took turns in front of the woman I said to myself: who did this woman belong to, that brought her here like this?! What enmity did they have with her or her father her husband or her brother?!

Dis honor able people …….this is the most cruel and barbaric behavior ………..where is the law now?!

The law book and all this writing should be hanged in the cell it was almost late at night there was a weak light inside the cell I looked towards the woman, there was no one next to her. Her long black hair fell on his face and shone in that weakly light I went to his side but I had you remorse I said: can I sit next you? She pushed her hair away with her hand I looked at her face and suddenly I felt like my whole being was on fire ………My God……. That woman was Nahid……..!! No……..It's not possible ……..!!

I wrapped her hair around my hand hatefully and shouted: No………..Nahid……..you are not even a flower of a swamp………..you are mud of a swamp……..

Breath Hold

The collar of my shirt was in Mikaeil's hands and he was slapping my face.

I opened my eyes more I was still shouting the sound of my scream was every were and several people were around me Mikaeil said aggressively: what happened again? I shouted: Nahid…….. where did she go?

Raouf who was standing a little away, said : who is Nahid?!

I yelled angrily: the same woman who was brought last night ……..!!

Sudden every one's noice was raised…. Which woman?! Did they bring woman last night?! Why didn't you wake us up?

Was she young? So you had a great time……..

Mikaeil said: Farhad, you had a dream last night I couldn't believe it……were they all asleep? I looked around myself Saeid was still beside me and his hand was in my hand I begged: Saeid………you tell me………. You overdosed last night you said that woman's voice was like morphine for you ………saeid looked at me with surprise and said with doubt: I …….?!

Did I say?! ……..I had overdosed?

Here?! Where is the woman……..?

I don't remember! Mikaeil shook his head and said to me: you don't want to ask him, he is confused ………he put a glass of water in front of my mouth and I drank a few sips ………he said again: Farhad you had a dream last night ………don't think about it I drank all the water in the glass and looked around again. I still doubted whether I dreamed or not I took a few deep breathes My God ……I had a dream no, it wasn't a dream it was a night more. Damn you Nahid……….

Breath Hold

I missed my daughter " Asl" in my mind, I
hugged and kissed her. I needed her a lot she smelled the freshness of
spring I looked at my hands…….they were empity, there was no one in
my arms…..God I entrust my daughter to you, take care of her Mikaeil
pulled my hand and said:

It's time for breakfast I wasn't good I could walk hardly I dragged my feet
on the ground Mikaeil? Yes dear…………

I wish they would execute me sooner I can't bear it anymore Mikaeil kept
silent and didn't say anything …….

I knew that he was upset I said again in a very sad voice: Mikaeil, it's good
that you don't have a wife and children……and he gave a sad smile if you
have been in prison you understand the meaning of sad smile………..

Also, words like: " freedom", "sun", " air", "breath", "laughter", " crying",…… prison is like a world between this world and the eternal world………

when you are in prison it's as if you are suspended in the air even" hell" is wished for you It was time to go to the yard I sat on a rock and smoked a cigarette I didn't want to see anyone and talk to him Saeid approached me and sat next to me.

He was about 24 years old he was a student of "Sharif National university" and one of the best people in the national university entrance exam Farhad …..? yes dear….. do you remember what you said that they brought a woman to the our cell… by remembering the last night mar, I got angry and rudely said: No……I had a night more he sighed loudly and said with despair: I feel so bad, Farhad……..

Breath Hold

He was young and my heart was burning for him unfortunately he was addicted to drugs although I was feeling bad I asked him:

" Is something wrong?

Do you even understand what I'm saying?

I was crying and said:

Do you know what will solve our problem? No …….just hanging……….both of our faces were wet from crying I wanted to make him feel better so I said with difficulty: Saeid, what was your university exam rank? I knew this question would make him feel better……he smiled and said:

Without talking any help from anyone, I got the third rank of the national university.

I was interviewed on TV and it was broad cast what made you come here? He wiped his tears and said: in the university, the smallest thing you do will be reported to the higher authorities it was supposed to bring some unknown martyrs to our university and bury them in the yard!!

Most of the students and even the university staff were against this we had no problem with the martyrs and we are proud of them and their courage especially the " unknown martyrs" they valuable for all of us but everything must be in its place the university isn't a cemetery!!

Breath Hold

It is also a few pices of a person whose identity is unknown burying these people in the university yard was a good advertisement for this system and regime these people had lost their lives for this country and this regime misused of their blood the use of martyrs to promote.

The system upset students they protested for several days successively some of my friends and I were leading the group the "information group" of our university, questioned us several times they threatened us but we didn't care they came to our houses in the middle of the night and arrested us they put us in solitary confinement that same night my mother had a stroke…..that was what they did:

torture …….interrogation…….solitary confinement I was sorry but it was useless …….. They had made me addicted ……..!

Does that mean you got addicted in prison?!

Yes……They injected me with morphine every day when I became addicted they injected less to torture me when I became completely addicted they took me from solitary confinement to prison the prison doctor also gave me methadone every few days.

One day, they give me drugs the next day they don't I'm tired, Farhad ……I'm tired of life ……I don't want to be free……. I just want to die ……..I had nothing to say I didn't know what to say to encourage him ……….we both just cried curse the pen if it doesn't write in prison what happened to prisoners ………… curse the pen if it doesn't write, the wish of each prisoner is death……. Curse the pen if it doesn't write how many students and elites were addicted and hanged because of "right speech".

Curse the pen if it doesn't write here, there are many people with AIDS and hepatitis curse the pen if it doesn't write here raping a prisoner is part of the prison law….. and curse the open if it doesn't write in this part of world "the punishment for someone who speaks the truth is only execution".

Breath Hold

Chapter: 14

I would like a set of suits for a wedding ceremony, please oh, congratulations. Thank you .Morteza was staring at my face what?!..........shave your beard I smiled and said:

What's wrong with my beard?

My dear, the family you are visiting they all have mustaches….none of them have beards are you taunting? Morteza said crossly: what do you mean?!

I said: I have heard so many taunts and sarcasms from everyone during this time, sometimes I don't know what I am saying ……..well, everyone is right ……..a tree without roost will quickly wither.

It doesn't become a tree at all, it remains the size of a bush and is up rooted by mind and rain a family without roots is the same……… Morteza, shut up please …….!

Because these aren't your words my father taught you to come and tell me this …….but I don't listen to you..

Breath Hold

Morteza was upset by my words, shrugged his shoulder and said: do whatever you think is appropriate……..

I put on my clothes in peru's room white shirt……

Black suit and black shoes do you think I should wear a tie?

No…..it's too formal Morteza ……..I have butterflies in my stomach don't talk like women why do you think like fools?

Well, we men heart too, this many happen to us well, tell me I 'm stressed…….this is better, more manly I rased on of my eye brows and laughed Morteza laughed too Morteza come with us too he waved his hand in the air and said:

thank you it's enough to get you. They were able to grab you.

Do you mean that you are praising me now?

He widened his eyes and said:" wouldn't you like me to praise you"? I shrugged my shoulder and said: any way they don't have another single girl, Nahid has a sister who is also married.

"Yes, I heard about her," he said sarcastically I said angrily:

You know I hate teasing we left the store I took Morteza to the car exhibition he was like my brother and worked for my father since child hood.

He works with me in the car exhibition several years ago, his father had died and he had been working since he was a child he had two sisters who were younger than him and my father took care of them very much I put my clothes on the couch my brother was very worried where is my father?

He went out.

Breath Hold

It was clear from my mother's face that she was very worried but on his face I loved this model of her face, it seemed to show her kindness and mother hood I hugged her and kissed Her and said I love you, mom……..

Her smile turned into laugter ………..

Mom, I 'm worried she didn't say anything what if my father doesn't come?

She said doubtfully: I don't know…..

The doorbell rang………he is your father ……..

Open the door I happily opened it when he came in, he was very upset hello father ……….

He shook his head and said something under his breath It was the end of September and my mother brought him a cool drink he tasted a little and put the glass on the table.

He looked at me and I was worried sudden, he turned to my mother and said loudly: you and Farhad go to Nahid's house I will not come I said:

Father, if you don't come, we will not go too…….he said sternly: tell them that I'm not satisfied with this marriage but I have no objection either my father was very angry if I said anything, bad something might happen I looked at my mother she was upset again …………I went to my room and smoked a cigarette.

I looked at my watch, it was exactly 8 o'clock Nahid and her family were waiting for us at a 9 o'clock …….. I didn't know what to do I could hear my father's voice saying: they say Nahid's father was a womanizer her brother is the same………

Breath Hold

My mother's voice could be heard more softly as she said:

"Darling......Nahid's father and brother's past isn't related to her my father shouted:

"Don't say this stupid words". Let your son know that her family isn't worthy of us I went out of my room and looked at my father I was very angry I wanted to shout like him and say that you promised me that we would go this weekend but I didn't say it and just looked at him and then left the house.

I wanted to call Nahid and tell her that we aren't coming tonight but I couldn't and I just sent her a massage " my dear Nahid I'm sorry, we can't come to night" she immediately called me but I couldn't answer and turned off my mobile phone.

I got into my car and left…….I didn't know where.

I was going I was going at a high speed ……maybe I wanted to crash and die if Nahid isn't in my world, I don't want that word I don't know how many hours I had driven, but I had reached the roads in the north of country but these roads were not familiar to me, I was in the middle of the forest.

I went further In one part of the forest there was a plain full of chamomile flowers in another part there were yellow flowers and colored lilies and in another part there were yellow and withe daffodils. I parked the car and lay down in the middle of the flowers It was like being in the middle of heaven I looked at the sky and shouted:

God, I don't want heaven without Nahid my hear beats fast the cool wind of September blows on my face and takes Nahid's long black hair everywhere I wanted Nahid's long hair and her big eyes to be mine at all love means Nahid's long and black hair love means big and lack eyes of Nahid.

Breath Hold

Love means the hands of Nahid, Nahid is mine because I love her I got up there were some huts in the plain.

I went to the huts a man wearing baggy black pants a while T-shirt and a straw hat was sitting next to one of the huts I greeted and he answered with his head I pointed to the huts and asked: are these for rent?

He said with 2 fingers of his hand and with a northern accent: 200 thousand tomans for each night how many nights do you want? For 3-4 nights we passed by a hut that was bigger than the others and had a big terrace.

I said if this cottage is empty, I will rent it the rent of this cottage is too much its not good for you it doesn't matter.

I will pay whatever it is we entered the hut together it had two small windows a small sink some plates were hanging on the sink some blankets.

Were stacked in the corner of the room the floor of the hut was covered with an old carpet there was a small stove with a kettle and a teapot on it several people rent here together you have to rent a small cottage I don't like the small space give me an ID card for what? The rental law is this …….I will bring it to you he gave me the key and left I opened the windows for fresh air…..

Breath Hold

There was a very beautiful view outside the hut I sat by the window and smoked a cigarette there was a narrow river after the chamomile flowers.

I was engrossed in watching this beautiful sight in my imagination I picked a bunch of chamomile flowers and tide them to Nahid's hair suddenly my hand burned with the cigarette butt, and I came out of my dream I was leaning on the iron bars of the cell and counted them every day the number of bars changed every day….! One day there were 14……..one day there were 15……..it's unbelievable but once there was one!!

Once whatever I counted didn't, end…! The number of bars was more than a thousand…….!!!

The bars were pushed a side four other people entered the cell the guard locked the bars and said: they don't stay here long, give them a place when he said this we understood that they were being executed I looked at their faces ……

How young and innocent they were.

They were about 23 years old and even 20 years old My God why should they be executed?! Raouf sat next to them Abbass said:

BBC (Raouf) got curious again what are you doing with them?

Arash said: he thinks, he is still a teacher and he can ask every one questions without paying attention to the others Raouf started talking to the newly arrived prisoners all four of them were university student they were speak hopelessly their name were:

Hessaam, Mohssen, Abolfaazl and Peymaan, Abolfaazl said: last night, they tried to force me to eat depilatory past!

Paymaan who was very young and had just grown mustache, said:

They gave me a piece of glass and told me to cut the evin in your hand!

Hessaam said sadly: Tomorrow they will execute all of us………Mohssen didn't say anything and he just cried.

Breath Hold

Raouf said:

You must have caused a disturbance in your university that they want to execute you quickly Abolfaazl said:

Auniversity where students cannot speaks freely isn't useful in case, we are no different from animals Peymaan said:

The university where girls do prostitution to support their expenses should be closed Mohsen wiped his tears with his hand and perssed his hand on his throat to stop crying, then he said: they want to execute us but instead they tell.

Others that committed suicide please each of you who was released from this prison inform the media that we were executed without any defense and without any trial Hessaam cried loudly he was scared he as very young he said between his tears: I don't want be executed who should I tell that I was wrong?

I want to live.

I know, my mother, Mehr banou, will die after my execution Mohssen said:

My father advised me to just study in university and don't care about what is happening around me but the fool didn't listen to him.

They were all scared but I was happy for them because they were executed early and didn't have the same fate as Saeid and me in prison is equal to addiction rape and humiliation before the off time.

The head of the guards entered the cell …….these names I will read read, have been sentenced to death………Mohssen Taghavi, Hessaam seraj, Abolfaazl Ghiyathi, Peymaan vafadost, and Farhad Fardin………..

Breath Hold

By hearing my name, the blood froze in my veins and I fell on the ground ……..I saw myself next to the gallows.

The rope was around my neck I shouted: finish it I heard a loud laghter It was the sound of Nahid's laghter, no………, maybe it was the sound of Sadiq……Babak was also happy with all his heart in the midest of all the laghter and happiness, the sound of someone crying was heard it was the sound of my mother.

Was also silentiy crying Asal was also crying loudly I couldn't bear her tears I pushed the stool moment mtarily and it was over………

I was friends were around me Raouf……..Mikaeil……….Behzad…….Sina……..Mehdi. I'm still alive…..there was something strange inside me it was much bigger and scarier (terrible) than the monster only executioners can understand each other's situation……..

They took us to the quarantine room I had accepted that the end of my life.

Would happen in this prison everyone dies in a way and my death is to be hanged I was crying a lot the prison worker was talking to us I could only see the movement of his lips and I didn't hear his voice he came near me and said:

If you need anything I will bring it to you I stared at his eyes he didn't seem happy at all my heart my heart was burning for him he saw the execution of prisoners everyday did they pay him for talking to the executioners?!

Told him: I want a pack of cigarettes, a pen and paper I wanted to just smoke until the last moment Hessaam was laughing loudly……….it was the laughter of death ……..I lit a cigarette I had a pen in my hand but I couldn't write.

Breath Hold

These are the last moments of my lfe….in prison.

I thought it would be the most difficult moments for me…..but I feel calm and I am sure that "death" is better than days in prison "father, my dear father, never forgive me, because I didn't think about your advices for a moment.

I wanted to experience and learn by myself but I never thought that some experiences are irreparable those experiences not only don't teach people anything but also take their lives my father I leave my daughter to you my dear mother forgive me and take care of my daughter but Nahid, I don't know what to say about you for me you were like a good smelling perfume that ran out too soon I don't know if you were my love or the mistake of my life?!

When I put the pen down my cigarette was extinguished I smoke my last cigarette was and gasped before I reached the gallows the prosecutor several guards the head of the prison the head guard two prison workers and a mullah were present I saw Bahrami I wanted to go in front of him and spit in his face.

I didn't even have the feel of spitting we went to the gallows they tied our hands from behind our feet were also tied at that moment.

I remembered the slaughter of sheep how they take their legs and give them water and then put a sharp knife in their throats here they didn't give us water and they tied the rope around our necks Hessaam.

Was still laughing loudly Abolfaazl called God and asked him for help Peyman was crying but no tears were flowing instead Mohssen was crying a lot the stools fell on after another and they were hanged their legs were moving strangely and their heads were going this way and that on the rope Hessaam's laughter could still be heard I don't know why they didn't push my stool to get rid of me.

I had a strange peace that to believe it, was hard for me the prosecutor said to the head of prison: why didn't Ahmad reza Rezaei's father come?

He should execute him (Farhad Fardin) himself as if the stool under my feet had to be pushed by the guard Rezaei's father so that the retaliation would be done properly.

Breath Hold

The head of the prison, Mr Mahdavi said: "Sir, an order has just been received from the higher au authorities that the execution of Farhad Fardin has been postponed"

Ahamdreza Rezaei's father protested to this "order" because he (Farhad Fardin) is known as" corruption in land and should be hanged in public.

They untied the rope around my neck and opened my legs and took me down from the gallows but I was like the dead I saw the people around myself as ghosts ....

I was executed, I don't need to oxygen, I don't breath at all ….these are all ghosts………. The angels of doom must come and take me to the hell I also see the fire ……….it must be to torment me…….sudden, I felt that I had wings and I was flying my parents were also with me I was happy and I don't see the fire any more ……we soared and went up ……….there was only light above I didn't see my parents again I connected to the light I felt good and I was free suddenly I lost my wings and fell quickly….when I opened my eyes I was in the quarantine room the prison worker was on top of me and she was pouring water in my mouth slowly.

Why are they doing the opposite?!

Do they slaughter first and then give wather ?

He opposite of slaughtering of sheep!! My yeys were half open I didn't know if I was dead or alive?

The nurse said:

you passed out on the gallows ……….I cried I was too tired I wanted to be released I was lying on the floor of the hut and smoking I missed Nahid a lot I promised myself that even if I lose everything I will get Nahid , if Nahid isn't mine, I don't want the world either …….I turned on my mobile phone my mom's messages arrived one after the other ……….

" Farhad……….where are you, my son?"

" Farhad ……….come back."

Breath Hold

"Farhad………..me and you father are married about you", " Farhad………why your phone is off?

" Farhad………..tell me something about yourself "………Nahid's massages came later ………"my Farhad……. There is no life without you"," my Farhad ……..without you I am a stranger here", " my Farhad…..without you I will die"…….. I was saddened by Nahid's worries, but my mother's worries were not important to me!

A mother should worry. About her child and this is very natural….

I quicly called to Nahid love is a strange thing……..!

It takes you to another world and can make you a different person…it changes your thoughts you are in your own world and suddenly a woman enters in your life and she be all your thoughts it was Nahid's voice.

Yes, my dear …….my Farhad.

I put the phone on the speaker to hear Nahid's voice louder and started singing :

I can live without others, but I can't live without you Nahid also sang with me:

I can't live without you, my Farhad I was crying and I said in a sad voice:

Nahid….I miss you……..Nahid……..we are belong to each other you are mine because I love you more than my life Nahid said sadly:

Come back …….I am worried about you ……..I miss you I will come back today …….I came back the same day I talked to my father in my mind and said:

Either you will come with me to Nahid's house or I will go alone I can't live without Nahid I had reached to home before sunset my mother hugged me and cried for a few minutes my father was lying on the couch I went forward and kissed him.

Breath Hold

Hello father he answered me slowly his face was sad.

I preferred Nahid to my parents my parents who worked hard for me to grow up …..I was a stupid person I hurt their hearts and souls.

I didn't know at that time that everything should be done in its own way and that hurrying isn't the right thing to do but I was in a hurry ………..

I forcibly convinced my parents to marry with Nahid I didn't choose the right method and upset my parents my mother said:

Your father has just been discharged from the hospital I looked at my father's face surprised his face was yellow and pale! I asked my mother with surprise: why?!

She said: he had a mild heart attack ………I was away from my father's couch I went close and sat on my knees next to the couch.

I held my father's hands father, are you upset with me?

He was silent I said immodestly again:

I……..I love Nahid father I cannot live.

Without her father said in a weak voice:

I am worried about your future father I will have a future with Nahid I have no future without her I saw tears in my father's sick eyes but I didn't care too much! I just wanted Nahid my mother brought me a glass of drink it was the last days of summer and the smell of autumn was very where I didn't like autumn at all, I was feeling sad when it was starting I was lying on the floor of the cell and smoking.

Breath Hold

I saw smoke rings look like ropes to me the iron bars opened with a sound and the head guard entered and said: Farhad Fardin.

I raised my head a little and looked at him go to the prison warden's room, Mr.Hojjat al-Islami I asked: has my death sentence arrived?

No, it isn't a death sentence, he has something else to do with you the life of death- row prisoners in prison is such that you are killed little and they don't kill you at once and they don't make you comfort table.

I had seen Hojjnt –al-Islami several times before he was the head of Evin prison that night the time of execution had come he was young about my age his beard had grown to near his eyes when you looked at his face you first saw beard then two eyes he was very tall and square- shouldered in general everyone is afraid to see him his front teeth were like the teeth of a board he had a harsh voice and spoke with a stutter.

I had heard in the prison that prison that he used to seize and he was a thug now I don't know how he became the head of the prison!

Who supported him to reach this position? But I know very well that in this country no one is in his right place a country whose university students are in prison the head of the prison the head of the prison must also be a thug….! I knocked on the door…….come in his voice echoed like a speaker as if several people are taking to me… I entered…..I didn't know that the prison has such big rooms ……..!

He pointed to me to sit down he sat in front of me and stared into my eyes he said: what beautiful eyes you have! It's a pity for you to be executed…. Then he laughed out loud I remembered Bahrami and understood why he wanted me……. He brought a glass of drink for me and said: " Drink"!

Breath Hold

I knew I had to drink:

He came forward and said:

Who said that sodomy is a sin?

If you ask me, I say it is like a reward …….it depends on when and where it is done to deter mine whether it is a sin or a reward do you even know what "sodomy" means?

It is taken from a tribe called" Lout" the mean of the tribe of "Lout" were homosexual the stupid men of this tribe didn't have sex with their beautiful woman and did this with men well, in that case they would sin from the way he spoke.

It was clear that he was slowly getting drunk …..he paurd a glass of drink for himself and put some white pills in each of our glasses and drunk unitil the end he said again: there are no woman here so "sodomy" is the right thing to do I drained my glass and I don't know how many hours I was in that damn room……. When I came out of the room, I just wanted to commit suicide.

I wanted to scream with all my heart, but I couldn't ……..my body was shaking I lay on the floor of the cell …..It was sleeping time to prison my only companion in these difficult moments was only cigarettes.

Cigarettes…….cigarettes……..my only motivation for life and for the future how quickly one's desires change.

How quickly motivation change's a few years ago, my only motivation for life was Nahid but now it is "cigarettes" I coughed from cigarette smoke

….

My mother came with a glass of water and gave me some water she opened the window the cool wind of September entered my room how much do you smoke! I didn't say anything because I had already said what I said.

Breath Hold

She sat next to my bed and said slowly:

I didn't understand when our life become chaotic ....!

I asked sadly: "Mom …….are you also against this marriage?"

I just realized that I didn't ask my mom's opinion about Nahid at all do you allow me to Disagree?

No my dear ……..I don't but try force anyone to do anything she paused and said: tell them that we are going on Friday I bought a ring for Nahid ……..

"I will never forget these damn memories" I hugged my mother tightly and pressed my face to her face.

I said: I love you very much you and Dad are my whole world but I also love Nahid and I want to live with her it was the first night of autumn I had a big basket full of colored roses in my hand and a big cake box was in my mother's hand we were in front of Nahid's house I rang the doorbell.

I looked at my father's face he was frowning a man with a thick mustache came to the door. Hello ….please enter he was Nahid's brother, Babak he was wearing a tight t-shirt to show off his muscles.

He had tattoos from his fingertips to his arm their yard was small A hall, about 12 meters with a narrow kitchen, was their whole house they also had a small toilet in the yard their house wasn't furnished and we sat on the floor and leaned on Dorsal's.

Arranged in a row my father frowned more Babak stared at me at me and as if he was bullying me in his mind the tone of his speech was like gangsters her father's face was wrinkled like a crumpled piece of foil……….

Breath Hold

His face was thin and his cheeks were bony he also had many lines around.

His eyes her mother had a kind face and it was obvious that she was suffering from our presence. My father looked down on all of them Nahid's way of dressing.

Was different from them she was wearing white pants a pink blouse and a hair band of the same color as her blouse it was clear that my father was not happy.

With coming here and he wanted the party wanted to and quickly so he said: these two people love each other it is better to start our conversation Sadeq, Nahid's father said: do whatever you want.

Babak, as if he felt offened rolled his eyes at me and my father and said: maybe we don't agree with this marriage at all …….my father quickly said:

If you are disagree we will leave Sadeq looked at Babk angrily which means: shut up and he said to Nahid: my daughter bring a cake for the guests ……he meant that we are agree……then he said to my father "Continue, we will listen……" "Damn money……….no I'd rather say, curse poverty………it always humiliates.

People I looked at my father he was proud and he spoke confidently but Nahid's father was silent it was as if he didn't dare to speak but Babak was rude I don't know who supported him who looked so arrogant!

Breath Hold

My father offered 500 gold coins? For marriage portion Sadegh looked at his wife and Nahid he humped more and said: the dowry of that one, my daughter is 114 gold coins, the same amount is enough for Nahid.my father said with more pride : how much should I give for "Shirba haa"? (shirbahaa means: a gift to a bride's mother for having nursed her/ bride price)(an old custom).

Shall I give cash? Tell me to draw a cheque.

I saw Nahid's eyes filled with tears but I didn't say anything It was obvious that Babak wanted to talk but Sadegh gave him a glare and didn't allow him to say anything his face was red with anger.

It was clear that he is putting pressure on himself out of respect for my parents Sadeq said: we don't have this old custom in the end Babak couldn't bear it and said angrily: it seems like you come to buy and trade? My father stared in to Babak's eyes and said angrily:

Yes, son.........marriage is also a kind of transaction there was a bad silence Sadegh said: I will give trousseau as much as I can with a contemptuous look at their house.

Hold items, my father gave a funny smile and said:

It isn't necessary Farhad buys everything himself my mother clapped her hands and poured some flower and small gold coins on me and Nahid's head and put a big and beautiful ring on Nahid's finger Nahid's eyes were still full of tears, but she didn't let them fall out I didn't know that I would have to pay for these tears and humiliation with my life I could see the anger and humiliation in each of their face "They say that unexpressed feelings never go away and come out in uglier ways later".

And I felt that night "Love " died aluong Nahid's feelings.

Breath Hold

Exactly in the middle of February, we had a magnificent wedding.

Celebration it was snowing heavily and it turned everything white we were all happy about this my father bought us a big and furnished house near their own house after the guests left.

We played in the snow with the same wedding dresses I felt like a prince who found Cinderella's shoe and found her after a whole search Nahid was even more beautiful.

Than Cinderella with her white and ruffled wedding dress she looked more like "Snow white" in the snow and with that dress I felt happiness.

With every cell in my body I looked into Nahid's eyes and said: "They say that if two people are supposed to get married even if all the people in the world are against their marriage those two will get married: "Because the universe wants it that way I wrapped my hand around her waist and we walked together in the snow I said: shall we make a snow man with this snow? Nahid was excited like a little girl and said:

Wow I love snow man …….shall we make one?

I said surprisly:

Now?

Yes ……what's wrong with it?

I shrugged my shoulders and said: ok…..let's make it

It was midnight, the small twin king lamps were in the yard

It is still snowing we were cold and couldn't complete the snow man I wrapped my hand around her waist again and we went inside.

Breath Hold

Chapter 15

Under the shower, I stared at the spoon that I had sharpened it's bottom. I said slowly: A spoon is going to kill me.

I was crying silently…….here I'm coming to the end…….what bad end!

Father, I wasn't a good son to you I made you feel ashamed even after my death I will case you shame my mother, my dear mother, they say "heaven" belongs to mothers it means that God loves you. Please God for forgiveness to me.

I was crying I closed my eyes and put the sharpened spoon on my neck artery and pressed a little my hands were shaking I couldn't control them I threw the spoon and sat in the corner of the bathroom and cried loudly I said to myself loudly:

Coward ……..coward…….

I shouted: execute me ………please relieve me………

The guard who was standing outside came into the bathroom after hearing my voice.

He had a very bad voice and told me: what has happened? Why are you yelling …….?

Come out of the bathroom ……..staying in the bathroom for too longtime made you crazy………

Cleaning is not suitable for people like you……….

I wanted to put that sharp spoon in his mouth to choke him forever

It was morning I was staring at the iron bars of the cell and counting ……..from the beginning to the end and vic versa……there were 15 at a time.

Breath Hold

Once there were thousands………once there were 100……! I don't know why it increased and decreased.

The head guard pulled the bars a side and said: "Its breakfast time ………go away …….everyone move one ……"

I was still looking at the bars.

He pointed at me and said: you …….Farhad Fardin …….go to the ward chief's room, Bahrami has something to do with you whenever I heard Bahrami's name, I would get a headache but ……..I'm not Farhad had Fardin ……….I……..I don't know who am I!!!

I said with a moan: I'm not Farhad Fardin .

Shut up ………get out ……. Move on.

I thought a little am I Farhad Fardin? Farhad was executed I saw him, myself

Sometimes my brain didn't work. I followed the head guard when we reached Bahrami's room, he went.

I knocked on the door a few times.

Come in.

I entered my body wasn't shaking as if its cells were dead.

He pointed with his hand stared into my eyes I liked the other way.

He said in a harsh voice: look at me.

I was afraid of him like a lamb afraid of a wolf I looked at him.

He brought his head closer and said slowly:

I want to make you escape from prison.

I thought he was lying ……I didn't say anything he said angrily:" Didn't you hear me?

I said slowly: thank you.

He said again with a loud voice:

Breath Hold

Stupid person, don't you understand what I'm saying? I want to free you from here

I didn't understand why he wanted to bother me.

I didn't know what to tell him to let me go.

I was looking suppliant at him to let me go he had a big mouth and his lips were like the lip of a camel he had black and crooked tooth that when he spoke, I felt like he was tearing my throat.

He pulled his chair closer and said: Did you believe that I want to make you escape, from here?

I just looked at him and said nothing sudden he shouted:

Don't look at me like a fool answer to me I was scared and said with a stammer:

What do I to say?

He sat down on the chair again this time he said softly: Ok.

He brought his head close and stared into my eyes with his piggy eyes I was afraid he said slowly and carefully: your father ……….Nader Fardin.

He paused to see my reaction……..

My ears perked up I was waiting for him to say the rest he continued a little more slowly: he paid me 2 bilion tomans to make you escape from here.

I didn't understand what he was saying, I just looked at him like a fool.

Suddenly he slapped my face hardly I didn't feel anything I said that my body cell were dead the gray cells of my brain were also dead sometimes I remember that I am Farhad……..sometimes I thought I was a sheep ……!

I wanted to baa………! I was waiting for my turn to be slaughtered……… sometimes I thought I was a serial killer and I said to the people around me: "I have killed one thousand and one hundred people" and I believed that I would kill this number of people I didn't know where these numbers came from…….!

Breath Hold

My brain commended me and I accepted I looked at his big lips again they were very ugly and disgusting he opened an energy drink for me and poured some white powder in it and said: Eat this to get out of this state of confusion I ate until the end I felt that my brain stated to work.

It was like my brain to come out of my mouth and explode I put my hands on both sides of my head and pressed I felt like flying it took.

A few minutes for my body to return to normal. He sat in front of me are you well?

I shook my head and said slowly: I'm fine what's your name and last name?

Farhad Fardin.

He pulled his chair closer closer and said slowly but firmly:

Listen carefully to my words. Your father paid me to escape from here he paused and said:

Did you understand so far…? Did you believe it? I felt that the cells of my body are coming alive one by one.

I said: I understand.

He stared at me with his piggy eyes and said: Before I tell you the escape plan, keep thin in your mind……

If you get trapped for any reason, you will not tell anyone my name if I' am known, I'll make you wish for death at any moment……… do you understand?

I murmured: I understand.

I was trying to understand and what he was saying…….

Is he telling the truth or lying?

What is his intention?

I was still thinking about his words when he continued: Today is Saturday you have to prepare yourself to escape by tomorrow.

Listen to me carefully between 3 and 4 in the afternoon, everyone is in the yard.

Breath Hold

Go to the toilet at 3:30 there are 15 toilets.

At the end of the corridor, enter the last toilets one of the walls of the toilet has a rusty iron door instead of a wall that door is closed with some screws which was one of the entrance and exit doors of the prison about 20-30 years ago.

That door has a small window which I will leave a screw driver behind it, for you only is have ten minutes to open the screws you must do this, quickly when you open the door, you will enter a covered corridor at the end of it, there is a way out of the corridor in 5 minutes.

At the end of the corridor is a small iron door when you arrive, knock a few times after opening the door, there is a black Benz waiting for you the rest of the plan isn't up to me just get out of there very fast you shouldn't get stuck……….do you understand?

If you get caught don't say my name. You got it?! All his movements showed that he was scared ……….I was scared too.

Even though I didn't believe his words compeletly, I had a commotion in my heart my legs were shaking and I couldn't get up.

Bahrami looked at my trembling legs and said: angrily: If you like this tomorrow you will definitely get stuck do you understand? If you do the thing I said correctly and on time you will definitely escape I got up from the chair and stood.

He gave me a small and white pill and said: Eat this a few minutes before 3:30 It removes stress, I went to the door with my trembling legs, sudden, he came near me and said: Remember don't tell anyone about this you got it? I said slowly: I understand.

Breath Hold

My brain was frozen I wanted to bang my head against the wall to get out of this situation I entered the cell one of the beds was empty.

I lay on it and smoked my hands were shaking I felt freedom I was talking slowly with my cigarette smoke rings: you know I'm going to be free......? Can I believe it?

Is it possible? Repeating these words makes my heart beat faster.

I put my hand on my heart and said: be clam………

Slowdown ……… freedom is near sudden bad thoughts came to my head if it doesn't happen ………? If he lied ……..? If………..If……..I held my head in my hands and pressed my body was shaking I warpped the blanket around myself tighter I don't know how many days I was here in prison, time doesn't move forward at all.

Days and nights are the same I started counting the seasons………Last year, I was arrested at the beginning of winter spring and summer are over I understood from the heat and the mosquitoes that they came and ended Autumn is over too. I understood from it's sad sunsets winter has started again can I see the spring season outside the prison?

Breath Hold

Can I see the sky, trees and rivers sun stars and rain outside the prison?

If I'm released from prison, I will build a hut in the forest ……..full of oxygen and fresh air……No, the hut also has walls I hate doors and walls I will build a hut without doors and walls It can be done ………..I will make it.

I was talking to myself and smoking that I felt Mikaeil's hand on my shoulder he sat next to me on the bed what's up bro?

I liked his voice It calmed me down and attracted me to itself I leaned on the bed and said: Mikaeil……. I 'm very stressed………I don't know whether to tell you or not…..

He looked at me and said:

Tell me…….. if I can, I will help you I said: I will tell you in the yard.

Is it so important? Yes, very important Ok. Mikaeil left the same thoughts came again I was going crazy I mean can I run away so easily?

I can't be alone……….I'd better tell Mikaeil so we can run away together if he accompanies We, I will be brave I remembred a few months ago ………. One of the prisoners had escaped through the big sewer pipes but a at that moment he was shot I'm not afraid of dying, but I was afraid that if I got caught "torture" , "interrogation", and "solitary cell" would be waiting for me, my whole body trembled at the thought of it.

Maybe, Bahrami wasn't to put me in solitary confinement so that he can do whatever he wants.

At 3 o'clock we went to the yard I sat in a corner and waited for Mikaeil he came and sat next to me while looking at the high walls of the prison, I said:

Mikaeil, can you believe it, Bahrami want's to escape me from the prison?!

Breath Hold

Shush!..........Speak slower …….tell me what happed exactly? I looked around, there was no one near us I said slowly:

In the morning I went to Bahrami's room. Well……..

I said very briefly: My father paid him to let me run away he said with especial excitement:" Who ……? How? Speak properly……….!!

He (Bahrami) said: tomorrow, have to go to the last toilet at 3:30 (pm) one of the walls of that toilet, is an iron door that is closed with screws he said that he will put a screw driver in the same toilet for me.

I have 10 minutes to open the screws then I pass through a corridor at the end of which is outside the prison and a car is waiting for me.

Mikaeil was surprised like me he was staring at my face he didn't even blink.

Mikaeil ……….do you think I should believe Bahrami's words?

What ……..? What did you say……..?

Before I could say anything, he continued:

Bahrami is a crud person and will do anything.

I asked with despair: do you think he is lying?

I don't know, I have to think, Mikaeil let's go together his eyes widened in surprise what.......? How ....? It's dangerous ....go yourself ......give me some time and let's go together his eyes widened in surprise what........? How.........? It's dangerous.........go yourself give me some time and let me think.

I said angrily: speak properly ....! I don't understand what are you saying.

My brain doesn't work Farhad, I don't understand what I'm saying he paused for a while and asked:

How much money he got from your father? Tow billion.

Did he say it, himself? Yeah

His eyes were wide in surprise he asked again:

Isn't he lying? I said with confusion I don't know ....I'm asking you.

Breath Hold

He looked at me without blinking then he said: can I come with you?

I took a deep breath and said: are you ok?

Just now, I said let's run away together.

Mikaeil was happy and said: can we run away together?

I don't know …….but it's better if we be together. Our courage increases.

He said: do you have a cigarette? I said with surprise: do you smoke?! Sometimes…… now I want a cigarette ……..

We both smoked in silence our minds were busy I knew we would be like that, until tomorrow. It was not easy ……

Until now, several people had tried to escape, but none had succeeded.

But it was different in my case everything was ready I took a deep breath ………again and again.

It was as if "lead" was entering in my lungs instead of air.

I felt suffocated. The screws couldn't be opened no matter how much I turned the screws, it wouldn't open It was as if hot melt had been poured on them……..I went to open the next screw it was just wrapped but didn't open.

Mikaeil …….Mikaeil…….where are you? Why don't you help?

No…..I'm afraid……….I won't come ………..go alone…….

Damn you………damn you……..

Suddenly the door opened I entered the corridor it was dark and I couldn't see anything I started running I ran and ran………when I reached at the front of door, Bahrami had arrived with several guards "Hojjat" al-islami" the head of the prison was also there they started laughing.

There were about to burst I decided to go back when suddenly the ceiling of the corridor collapsed.

Breath Hold

And I was buried under a pile of dirt help..........help, I'm suffocating, I'm going to the grave a live wakeup.......wake up, Farhad. It was near morning said was on top of me and shaking me. I opened my eyes completely and said to him:

Well I woke up my heart is still beating fast what a bad night mare it was my throat was dry I said to said:

Can you bring me some water? He went gropingly in to the darkness and came back with a glass of water I drank all the water and took a few deep breaths every moment my heart beat increased when we went for breakfast, I sat next to Mikaeil he said slowly: I gave up and will not come.

I put a piece of dry bread in my mouth and without looking directly at him (because there is a camera installed on every wall of the prison dining hall and the prisoners are being checked constantly), I said: why? Are you scared?!

No, I wasn't afraid I don't want your escape plan to fail It's better if you be with me.

We didn't talk anymore and I ate dry bread with tea time was passing too late for me.

Every second would take me a thousand years not only my heart but all the cells in my body were struggling with my gaze, I said goodbye to all my friends as well as to the walls and every bar of the cell door.

Will I don't see these bars tomorrow morning? What if I get stuck ……..? No………no……..I will definitely run away tomorrow "I felt freedom with all my heart.

The guard moved the bars and said: go to the yard I was stressed I felt fear stress and happiness inside myself". I wanted to laugh out loud.

No, I wanted to cry I didn't know what to do……..

Breath Hold

I didn't know if Mikaeil would come with me or not ………If he comes with me, I will get more courage I feel that I have a better chance to escape with him I was in the yard It wasn't yet 3:30 pm the pill that Bahrami gave me, was in my fist my heart was beating fast I felt Mikaeil's hand on my shoulder I quickly turned to him and said slowly: Damn you, where are you………..?

He sat next to me an said slowly: I'm afraid that if I come with you, a problem will happen to you I said firmly: I want you to be with me with you, I get more courage he took my hand and said:

With God's help, we will get out of this hell together it was a few minutes to 3:30.

I said: I'm going you come soon just be careful that the guard doesn't see you we both go to the same toilet I went to the bathroom 2-3 people were there the guard was also outside the bathroom corridor my heart rate was at 1000! I took the pill and calmed down without attracting attention, I entered the last toilet.

I looked for a screws driver behind the window and found it now I was looking for the screws to open them. The iron pate was covered with dirt I removed the dirt with my hand but it was dry I found a screw that was rusty and big I hope this screw driver will open it on the screw but it doesn't turn.

Breath Hold

It was hard as a rock where was Mikaeil? Why didn't he come? He must be scared……

I tried my best it was a little loose and then it opened I was looking for the next screw I removed the dirt and saw another rusty screw………

Where are you Mikaeil? Why didn't you come?

Maybe the guard has come into the corridor …….what will happen if he doesn't come?! It's okay, I'll go myself the second screw was easily.

Opened I was stressed I don't know how much time I had the upper screws were opened, but I couldn't find the lower ones dried mud covered them I poured water to make it a little soft, then I used my nails to removed the mud, but I couldn't find it I poured water again and removed the mud with my nails my fingers were injured I was loosing the screws with a screw driver when Mikaeil entered I said slowly: where have you been? Why are you late? He just said under his breath: shush!

He quickly took a screw driver and removed the screw I don't know how much time we had, we didn't say anything as the sound of our breath was complicated in the bathroom we also found the last screw but it was damaged and couldn't be opened completely we were both tired the iron plate was loose, we shook it and the screw came out.........

We put it aside slowly there was a narrow and dark gap I entered first and then Mikaeil came as we went forward the gap got bigger.

We reached a corridor when we raised our heads they hit the ceiling and there were walls an both side of us It was clear that it was a narrow and small corridor we ran in a stooping posture ....

As if this damn corridor had no end we didn't dare to speak and just ran sudden my head hit an iron door I said happily: It's over ....yes, it's over I knocked on the door and it opened after a few seconds.

Breath Hold

The door was very small we bent down more and came out a man who covered his face with a black cloth was behind the door he pointed to the car and said: get in very fast Mikaeil fell to the ground and was thanking God Mikaeil what are you doing? Get up……..we don't have time.

The car was parked about 15 meters away, on the as phalted road, and as Bahrami said, it was a black Benz we ran and got into the car.

The driver was waiting in the car as soon as got into the car, the prison alarm sounded that sound was because of our escape I yelled:" hurry up…….move."

The sound of our heart beats filled the car when we were completely away, Mikaeil said:

When we were completely away, Mikaeil said: did we really run away? I cannot believe……

I looked at Mikaeil and couldn't say anything I just laughed out loud then I cried and shouted: we ran away ……….God thank you ….and then I put my head on Mikaeil's

Shoulders and we cried together.

The windows of the car were completely dark and the driver was almost the same age as me and was driving at a very high speed he looked at me from the mirror and said: I thought I had to let someone we just looked at him and said nothing he asked again: which one of you is Fardin?

I am he didn't say anything and went into a dirt road that was village a black Peugeot was parked on the side of the road and said:

Breath Hold

You have to go the rest of the way with this car where should we go?

As they told me, you are going to the border at night and enter turkey from Urmia, which has already been coordinated with the smuggler.

 I just had to take you here from the prison he gave me a bag of clothes and said: :before you get off, change your clothes a jacket a shawl and hat and a bunch of bills, which all of them were traveler's checks before I said anything, he said: snow was arrived at the border and it's very cold you have to cross the border on foot 10 million is the cost of your trip.

Be careful there are many thieves and smugglers on the way, they easily kill people for a traveler's check I looked at Mikaeil and said to the driver: so, what about my friend?

A man who was covering his face took off his mask and said: I will give him my clothes.

He quickly took off his clothes so that only a short and underwear were left on him.

Mikaeil said: you are very kind thank you ther driver also gave his jacket to Mikaeil.

Thank you so much ………people like you are encouraging then we quickly got into the Peugeot and left the Peugeot driver grumbled: "you came too late"

The speed of the driver was too high I don't know if he knew anything about us or not?

Mikaeil said: where are we going to go?

The driver looked at us from the mirror and said: I was told to take someone to Urmia and deliver him to the smuggler I didn't know there were two people!

Breath Hold

He said again: did you escape from prison?

So he knows………..yeah he looked at us from the mirror, blinked a few times and said: escape from Evin prison isn't for everyone I hope you didn't get stuck.

Mikaeil said: we will hot get stuck the driver said: the smuggler was paid for one person I hope he agrees to let both of you cross the border I said: we can call our parents and tell them to deposit the money he quickly said: No, never do this the police will check your family's phones to find you.

He was right I hadn't thought of that I still couldn't believe that we escaped ………had we really come out of that hell?!

I looked around eagerly It was as if I was reborn.

I was very excited and wanted to see my daughter and my parents sudden, I felt that I was in my mother's arm's we were both crying Nahid was looking me but I turned away from her I opened eyes, we were in the car Mikaeil was looking at the sky and smiling. It was night and we were all silent in the car No one was in the mood to talk the lights of Urmia gave us hope the driver said: we will be in Urmia in half an hour.

Breath Hold

I was very hungry I wanted a delicious and warm meal but we didn't dare to get off the car It had snowed and everything was white it was still.

Snowing sporadically and under the light of the lamps, it was dancing on the ground life..........the world and nature are beautiful thank you God for giving me anther chanc to live when you go to the gallows, you understand how beautiful life is we arrived in Urmia at 11pm the driver parked and truned his head back his eyes were round and black they were very black his hair was bristly as if he had been electrocuted he said: I will go and buy some sandwiches don't get off would you like a drink?

Yes thank you when he left , I lowered the car window a little everywhere he left was quite it was as if the city had gone into hibernation under all that snow.

Does that mean we can cross the border? With God's help, we will pass I hesitantly tell me bro said: Mikaeil , can I ask you a personal question?

Even though you aren't a Muslim, you believe in God and call his name he smiled meaning fully and said:

You know ……..you Muslims think that only you worship God no, you are wrong we also worship God I have seen many Muslims who see to worship God but never follow his words but prophets to everything does that mean you also accept the prophets?

God messengers…………Abraham Moses, Buddha, Zoroaster, Christ and Muhammad are our prophets I asked shyly: then why they say that you are impure?

Breath Hold

I didn't continue and quickly said: I'm sorry, I never accepted this but I understood that he was upset he said with a sad voice: do you every one worships God in his own way. In my opinion, no religion should condemn the another then he read some verses of Rumi's poems. After that his tears flowed I hugged and he said:

I wish there would be a time when accepting "religion" isn't compulsory anywhere in the world and one will be imprisoned for religion.

I wish, religion isn't a tool to rule kill, and bully I wish there will be a time when "humanity" is the first word of all religions.

The driver returned with 3 sandwich and 3 soft drink and said: "eat quickly" we have to go to sarv border road I will deliver you to the smuggler there.

They leave at 12 Am Mikaeil said: about half on hour I smelled the sandwich I really liked sausage before I went to prison I was never allowed to eat sausage sometimes I ate secretly and outside the house I ate very quickly due to hungry Mikaeil was the same.

The driver didn't talk white driving as if his concentration was lost.

Exactly after half an hour we reached the sarv road there was a small border town. He stopped near the bazar and called someone.

Hello………Qasseme……….? He paused a bit and said: I'm calling from Fardin we are next to the bazar.

Breath Hold

He said again: Ok, we are waiting he hang up the phone and said: someone is coming to pick you up now soon a car parked behind us and signaled with it's lights.

The driver said: It's him, go we said goodbye and left we hadn't gotten into the car yet when the man rudely again: Get on!! The driver's head was bald and he had a big mustache he blinked a few times and said: "I have been arranged for one person." Which one of you is Fardin?

It doesn't matter, let both of us cross the border he said angrily: "It isn't possible ……crossing the border of two escapees from prison is very dangerous." Do you know the crime of someone who helped you? Execution…….

Damn you! How do you know that we escaped from prison?

Mikaeil was worried and said: what is the problem?

The man touched his mustache and said: my problem is money………I took money for someone I quickly asked: how much money 5 million I accepted.

Breath Hold

He said: let's go and moved Mikaeil wanted to say thanks, but I said: mikaeil, you are like my brother, you are my dear Mikaeil was happy and smiled: when we went a little further, the smuggler said: we have to take a path on foot.

A van is waiting for you when you pass the Turkish border post we get out of the car. It had snowed a lot there were two other smugglers with several men and a 20 – years –old-girl.

It was very cold 4 of those men were from Afghanistan, two of them were from Pakistan two of them were young Iranians who were about 21 years old and their beards and mustaches had not yet grown.

They were thin and weak their faces were pale I don't know if they were like that because of the cold or if they were scared the situation of the girl was the worst her hair was hidden under her hat and a scarf was wrapped around her neck she was about 23 years old. What is a girl doing among all those men near the border?!

Does her family know? Maybe she didn't have anyone when I looked at her my heart was pounding she had beautiful eyes it had been a long time since I had seen a woman.

The other men looked at her a lot she was left like a piece of meat among hungry wolves when I looked at her, my blood pressure rose and my heart beat faster and my frozen blood was flowing.

Breath Hold

3 smugglers were with us and they ecoureged us they said: if you wait a few more minutes and the situation is right, we will enter Turkey as they traveled along this route, they knew all the places very well. Cold said to Mikaeil: I'm very cold……I am freezing suddenly, one of the smugglers turned his head to words me and angrily said: shush………! Be quite my smuggler, who was bald, appoarched and said softly: don't talk to each other and don't smoke at all.

The other two smuggler were tall and walked ahead of the others we were on the road for about 2 hours my legs were numb and my face was red like everyone else because of the cold.

I looked at that girl, I left that she was crying her hand was under her eye maybe something Went into her eyes the mobile phone of one of the smugglers rang we all looked at him he didn't say anything and just listened his face.

 Become sullen and he said sadly: we have to go back, the Turkish border guards are on duty we were unable to speak and protest because of the cold we couldn't open our mouthes two other smugglers also came back and said: we have to go back down so that the situation will be normal.

There was a village at the bottom of the mountain there were several scattered huts in the village we were divided into three groups the girl went with one of the smugglers six other people who were Afghan and Pakistani went with another smuggler as if the return way was more difficult.

Breath Hold

When we were going up, we were hopeful now we are returning with disappointment we didn't know what was waiting for us.

The snow had melted and the mountain was dark and cold there was snow everywhere we entered the village hut there.

 Was no water or electricity there was only an old heater in the corner of the hut which was enough for all of us.

 We sat around it to warm up but the weather was very cold sudden, one of the boys started crying after him, his friend also cried Mikaeil and I had suffered so much in prison these kind of problems didn't make us to cry Mikaeil hugged one of the boys and said:

This way you will warm up better I also hugged that one boy I asked: what's your name?

Behzad.

That one boy also said: my name is Mehran how old are you?

We are 20 and 21 years old. Mikaeil said: why do you want to leave Iran? Why do you go like this? Is there no place for you in Iran?

Behzad said with a lump in his throat: I have been working since I was a child after finishing primery school, I didn't go to school anymore my father was a pedlar and I used to work with him one day, a municipal employee kicked my father's side.

Breath Hold

He also tooke the items that we had arranged for sale with himself since that day, my father couldn't work and his kidney was damaged.

He had urinary incontinence we had no money to treat him all the capital of our life was the few scarves and T-shirts that man took with himself and never returned.

From that time, I didn't everything I used to carry goods in the market, wash toilets and clean shop windows my father died two years.

Later his kideys were infected and we had no money of his treatment I had two sisters who got married I was living with my mother who also died last month I have no future in Iran I'm tired of doing so much work but it didn't benefit for me......... he cried again and Mikaeil was caressing his head I said to Mehran: why are you leaving? He had stopped crying and his head was on my legs.

He said: like Behzad and thousands of other people who have no hope of life in Iran, Iran away we are all the same, but our we are all unemployed , we all have no money, we don't have a place to sleep and a hot meal I grew up in " Halabi Abad" my father was an addict and I hadn't mother I don't know if she was dead or divorced I never saw her I had a brother was also addicted my sister also married someone like my father I was always hungry I can't sleep at night because of hunger no one helped us all the laws to protect of children, drug addicts and families are, lies sometimes they would come and take some photos and videos of our living conditions and leave but no one ever helped us.

He started crying again……….

Mikaeil said:

Breath Hold

I wish, instead of dealing with issues as whether the people are Shiites or sunnis or Christians, the "Iranian" system would think about the "people" themselves its leaders should think about eliminating " poverty" and "addiction" Iran " is drowned in poverty and addiction I was thirsty In the corner of the hut there was pitcher of water and a glass I poured a glass of water and drank it.

Suddenly there was a sound from the ceiling everyone looked at the ceiling I quickly went next to them and said slowly: it seems like someone is walking on the roof Mikaeil said: there must be a jackal.

He said so that we shouldn't be afraid but, it was the sound of feet we were all silent and staring at the running on the roof.

Behzad was scared and was clinging to me Mikaeil said again: don't be afraid ………maybe a cat got stuck there I said angrily:

What are you saying?! There is a sound of footsteps we heard the sound of several shots being fired from outside there was a hole behind the oven where the smuggler told us to hide in, if we felt in danger Behzad and Mehran hide in the hole and Mikaeil and I stood by the door so that we could defend ourselves if someone entered no sound could be heard after the shooting everywhere was quiet.

The shadow of the fire fell on the wall and became like a monster sometimes it was small and sometimes it was big it had big mouth it was as if it was laughing with the bursting of fire wood and saying that this hut is your coffin you will die here.

I leaned against the wall and sat down Mikaeil said slowly: shall we go out ……..? let's see what happened ……..! No….it's dangerous!

Mikaeil didn't pay attention the door opened with a sound like a moan Mikaeil first put his head out and then left himself I also went behind him.

A little further, two bodies were lying in the snow.

Breath Hold

Red blood had colored the snow of around them the shadow of two people could be seen coming towards the hut in the darkness we quickly returned to the hut I pointed to Behzad and Mehran, who had come out of the hole, to go back there.

Those two people were right behind the door of the hut my legs were shaking and I couldn't breathe one of them opened the door a little and put his head inside and said: come out quickly we should go he was one of our own smugglers we had peace of our mind we all left quickly before we could ask a question one of the smugglers pointed to the corpses and said:

They are smuggling "humans" if you were caught by them, it would be impossible to save you I don't know why I didn't believe their wards it must have been a personal enmity it was near the morning and it had started to snow again a little further, the other started to that girl was also with them when I see her, it is as if the blood flows in my body.

Damn this "sense", that was found in me in this situation.

I wasn't an ogler man. I don't know, maybe it's the result of prison. Prison changes peoples identity I know very well that I'm not that Farhad before of prison. This new Farhad was a stranger to me.

We were all given white clothes white hats and white shawls the smuggler who was the youngest and tall, said: camouflage yourself in these clothes so that, only your eyes are visible you may have to cross the border by crawling.

The sun had risen It was around 7 am the weather walking again in the snow we were all hungry they give us biscuits I looked at the girl again it was o'clock in the morning we couldn't walk anymore one of the smugglers said:

Breath Hold

We rest a little further there was a hole in one of the foothills we all entered it was warm there we sat but were not allowed to talk the person sitting to me put her head on my shoulder.

I thoiught it was Mikaeil I wanted to say something when I saw that person is the same girl I left my heart is coming out of my chest they again give us some biscuits with milk.

It was very dry and bad-tasting I could feel the shaking of the girl I don't know if it was from the cold or from fear I also trembled.

A strange feeling shook me that it didn't relate to cold or fear she said slowly: could you held my hand ……..? It's frozen ……

I was just looking at her she brought her hand closer.

I took her delicate hands it was like a piece of ice! I took it near my mouth and started to "ha" to warm it up Ha ha ha ha ……..

A strange heat was coming out of my mouth I came to myself and saw that I was kissing her hand. It was between my hands and my warm lips I was kissing back to back.

A few Pakistan men were staring at us I felt bad I wanted to blind them their eyes were greedy they didn't even blink.

I took the girl's hands away from my lips Mikaeil hit my shoulder ………get up ……..they say come out I got up and the girl's hands were released from my hand.

Warm blood flowed inside my body I looked at the bottom of the hole……

There were several skeletons ……… It must have been for a cot or a dog……….No!

My God it was a human skeleton!………. The skeleton of the head, legs and chest………

Breath Hold

I stopped breathing because of fear while I pointing to the skeleton, I said to Mikaeil: look there!! He said by coolness: yes ………I saw.

We came out of the hole one by one of smugglers, while the with ness of the snow was bothering his eyes, said slowly: in a few seconds, the Turkish border guard will leave his post, it will take 5 minutes for him to come we have coordinated with next military police, you must cross the border quickly in this time.

He looked at the Turkish border guards and quickly said: Hurry up……… go in a stooping posture and stay away from each other as soon as the shot id fired, lie on the ground and don't move.

He pointed and the Afghans and Pakistan is separated after them, two Iranian boys, a girl me and Mikaeil were last ones.

We went in the same way as the smuggler said I was very stressed I was waiting for the shot every moment these few minutes have passed for us as many years many were killed by the Turkish border guards on this route.

I remembered the words of Mehran and Behzad: "we are ready to die at the border, but we will not return to Iran it was thousand times better to die than to return".

I was very stressed we had been going for ten minutes we had crossed the border but we were still in danger the smugglers told us: stay as for away from the border as you on the other side of the border.

We reached a rock and climbed up we had to slide a part and jump down we jumped on by one the girl fell on the snow and didn't move it was as if she was dead I fell next to her.

Breath Hold

I put my hand on her pules it was beating………I was beating …….

I heard Mikaeil's voice: Is she alive? I said under my breath: yes, she id alive I slowly put his hand on my lips my lips were frozen I kissed her hand one after the other I felt that the blood flowed in the veins of her hand……….it became.

Warm………warmer………

Mikaeil helped he lifted the girl up and said: "Farhad, get up, we fell away from the others".

We have to get ourselves to the van with Mikaeil's help, we lifted up the girl and started waking.

We saw a white van in the distance we were very happy, but we could hardly walk very the van and were waiting for us.

When I got near the van, I fainted Nahid runs towards me. She opened his arms for me and was laughing I was crying.

Sometimes I heard laughter and sometimes the sound of crying sometimes the sound of Asaal was heard as she laughed.

She opened her arms to me, I had opened my arms to her I hugged her she smelled like" orange blossom". Sometimes I could smell the bitter smell of life…….I kissed her a thousand times………..one after another ……..sudden, the taste in my mouth went astringent…….like the taste of an immature persimmon my tongue stuck in my mouth ………..suddenly I saw Nahid………

I moved back ………..she wasn't laughing anymore……… she was crying ……….her tears were red like blood…………her eyes and face were red.

Blood was dripping from his face I shouted: Nahid, get out of my life……..Nahid, I hate you…… Farhad …………are you Ok.

I opened my eyes a little Mikaeil was next to me. I looked around ………we were in the van I asked surprisely: Does that mean we crossed the border? Does that mean we ran away?

Mikaeil said with a smile: " yes, bro……."

It's over then laughed ………I laughed with him.

Breath Hold

While he was laughing, he said: you will be my brother forever we hugged each other people don't hug each other just for "love" there are many reasons to hug other that sometimes it's pleasure is more than love.

We reached the city of "van" they took us to a ware house the van driver said: stay here and we will inform you. Those six people who were Afghan and Pakistani didn't come with us they had arranged with a smuggler in Istanbul to go to Greece from there they brought us a food that looked like "Abgoosht" (It's an Iranian stew It is also called Dizi)

Broth due to extreme hunger, we ate quickly inside the ware house was the smell of sewage Me, Mikaeil, that girl and two Iranian boys were in that dirty ware house for about 24 hours.

They scared us a lot and no one dared to come out we used to sit on a carpet and sleep.

The carpet was very rough and dry the girl opened her that and shawl she opened her hair which was tied with a barette on top of her head her hair fell down to her waist like a water fall I was just staring at her hair and face and her slim body It was very beautiful and lovely I said to her: what's your name? She said: Sara.

I said: your name is as beautiful as you are Mikaeil said: It's very dangerous for a single girl to cross the border by smuggling why did you do that?

She leaned against the wall and said: I had to come smuggled I asked: Did your parents die?!

Breath Hold

She paused she looked at each of us and said: yes……..they died a few moments later she came near me she sat next to me and said slowly: my father died two years ago he had cancer it wasn't long before, I found out that my mother was in relationship with my father's friend. When I protested to my mother she said: I nursed………you will get married and I can't live alone I said: I wish you had waited longer my father just died ………..why did you marry with my father's friend?! My father is sad………

She said indifferently: you don't understand me I really didn't understand her……… but she didn't understand me too.

She was my mother and she destroyed all my feelings I couldn't believe that a couple could forget each other so easily after living together for several years.

Since then, I kept quiet and didn't say anything to her but all the bad thoughts came to me sometimes when I thought too much my hands and feet trembled it was very difficult but I had come to terms with fact that she got married I had no choice.

I told my mother: don't let anyone know about this, for at least a year she agreed, but forgot after a while she was always out with Homayoun (my father's friend).

Everyone was talking about them I decided to tell everyone the truth the contemptuous look of the others bothered me I endured everything but it didn't matter to my mom.

Homayoun came to our house whenever he wanted when he came, my mother would say: Go out for a few hours were I should I go?

I don't know you have so many "friends" go to one of them's house my mother was the one who didn't allow me to go to my friend's house until my father's death.

Breath Hold

U know? When life conditions are good and normal, everyone is good and feels responsible but when their interests are endangered, they destroy the sense of responsibility, even the sense of mother hood whenever Homayon came to our house, I felt like I was being tortured.

One morning when I was still sleeping sudden, I saw Homayoun above me I panicked and asked: where is my mother?

He laughed stupidly and said: she is not at home and has gone out then he shamelessly asked me for sex.

U know?

I love you so much I slapped him hard on his face ……..so hard …….that he fell to the ground it would serve him right I said: I haven't seen a creature as you as you.

That asshole man just laughed I came out of the house when I explained the matter to my mother she said: these are the products of your mind you want to ruin my life.

I will buy a house for you, go and live alone I don't know how, they appropriated my heritage with Homayoun It seems that all the properties have already been transferred to my mother.

I left home forever and lived with one of my friends my mother sometimes deposited money in my back account I couldn't stay in Tehran she was a stranger to me I killed her forever in my heart I wanted to cross the border legally they said: you need your mother's permission to leave the country I didn't want to talk to her either I decided to smuggle.

Sara's hands were in my hands. I didn't understand when she did this her hands was cold like ice she said slowly: can you hold my hands worries me.

I said involuntarily: Sara …….I love you she said slowly I love you too I didn't say anything I hated the word "love" I wanted to bury this word forever.

Breath Hold

Someone entered the ware house he wasn't familiar he spoke in Turkish, he indicated that we should follow him we boarder a van again one of my friends was translating his speech and said: we are going to go Istanbul from there we will be on our own, we must be careful don't to arrest the police I didn't know what to do next I wondered why my father didn't come to Turkey himself! Or at least he would send someone to help me what will happen if the police arrest us here?

I have nothing with myself …….. No passport………no brith certificate………nothing.

I will definitely be deported or imprisoned in Turkey everyone was afraid of the police because we entered this country illegally……

We were all stressed I was sitting next to Sara and Mikaeil and Sara's hand was in mine I said to Mikaeil : what if we get arrested? He said: Trust in God. But he was also worried you could see how worried he was from his face.

The journey was very long ……..long and tiring ……..I don't know how many times I fell asleep and woke up.

Due to stress and fear everyone was silent and didn't speak sometimes the driver and that stranger man spoke together in Turkish.

Turkish music was played inside the van and the driver sometimes sang along with the singer It was clear that he enjoyed listening to the song I was jealous of him how easy and fear less he lives and enjoys listening to music I don't think, I enjoyed listening to a song so much before I was imprisoned I didn't enjoy the moments of my life those moments just passed.

It wasn't my fault, we were never taught how to enjoy our life in any situation and in any place.

We were only thinking about the future.

The future tomorrow ………damn the future that always destroyed our moments if I get out of this predicament I won't live like before.

Breath Hold

I teach my daughter to live in the moment and enjoy it don't destroy the moment because of her future damn the future ....I want several children to play together and laugh out loud I want to comb and braid my daughter's hair.......then attach small colored clips to her hair Sara gently hit my shoulder and said: what are you doing?

Why are you pulling my hair?!

I looked at my hand .....Sara's long hair was in my hand .....

I looked at Sara's face a bitter smile appeared on my lips I had lost my life I hadn't lived at all God, give me another chance.

 I want to live I wish I could sew "smile" on the lips of all the people in the world finally we arrived in Istanbul I don't know, why I had a bad feeling I had no hope. When we got out of the car, the Turkish-speaking man said something in Turkish, which our friend translated again.

He says that this is the "Zeytinburnu" area in Istanbul there are many
people who entered Turkey illegally you can get help from them or go to
the country you want, from here it was very cold our faces were bruised
from the cold there was a bridge near us someone said: let's go under the
bridge.

When we reached the entrance of it, there was a large crowd
women………children……men……young people my God all these
people entered a stranger country illegally!

We were staring at the crowd everyone had a bay…..

I suddenly remembered my bag why was my hand empty? I looked
everywhere but my bay wasn't there I said to Mikaeil: my bag is lost he
said: be calm………

Think carefully, where did you put it?

In the car …….I put it in that damn car Iran around a bit Sara said: as soon
as we got off, he left.

Breath Hold

I said to Mikaeil: all my money was in the bag......... we have to look for the bag.

A strange Iranian man was near us and heard our words, said: this is useless ....even if you find it, you will not be able to get your money back.

I shouted angrily: why???? Why can't I get it back?

Because you are here illegally they also know this well and threaten to expose you to the police so you would have to say nothing and don't look for your money.

I was very angry and I was cursing myself: "you are a fool.........it's better that you die.........you couldn't take care of a bag "I sat on the ground Mikaeil said: what are you doing?

Get up..........the ground is cold.........it's Okey ....getup Sara sat next to me, massaged my shoulders and said:

I have some money don't worry" I was staring at her beautiful face her eyes were green they shone like two beautiful emerald stones I felt that they were blue yesterday………I also felt that they were gray!

Are you ok Farhad?

What did you stare at? I stared into your eyes she smiled and said: "of course you are fine get up she was saying right I was feeling better I got up from the ground men are phenoms that are unknown even to themselves I rudely looked at her eyes again and said: did you know that your eyes change their color?

Her smiled more and said: my father used to tell me that your eyes are like marbles I held her hand firmly in my hand and said: Sara whatever happens………you are mine……..remember this……..you are mine she laughed and said: yes…….

Breath Hold

Suddenly, there was an up roar in the crowd someone was feeding people Mikaeil surprised and asked the same Iranian man: do they give free food?

He said: there are same Iranian philanthropists who sometimes come here and feed people they know that the people here are hungry and have no money for food.

I was hungry too I asked, will we get food too?

He said: yes……..there is too much food a few minutes later, they came towards us. The food was sandwiches which I ate all of them with gusto we met a few people under the bridge no one wanted to stay everyone wanted to cross the Turkish border and go to another countries some of them were going to Greece……some of them Germany……….the countries of Bulgaria, Sebria, Great Britain, and Netherland were the rest of their choices Hamed was about 35 years old. He wanted to go to Greece by sea with his pragrant wife and his child his daughter was 5 years old.

His wife wasn't well why did you come with this condition of your wife? "Fear……..crossing the sea ……….fake identity".

I taught physics in university I class, the discussion became political and led to the protests of the Iranian people in 2008 I said: this regime must answer for this killing and answer for the imprisoned student too……..the political debate escalated and the order of the class.

 Was disrupted when the class was over the university security asked me they told me: because you disrupted the order of the class, you have to introduce yourself to the intelligence organization, until the next 24 hours. One of my colleagues, who was also one of my friends, said: leave Iran at night if you go to the intelligence organization, you will never come back now, I have been here for a week.

I looked at his pragrant wife and his daughter surprisedly I said: so you came here by land?

We came by air, but we got stuck here Mikaeil was standing on the bridge and was getting information from the others I went near him he said: Farhad if we want to leave here, we need money, we have to find a job.

Breath Hold

How to find a job? We live here illegally a man who was near to Mikaeil and was listening to our words, said: my name is Erdogan. My friend needs a worker he speaks Persian well.

Mikaeil continued: we work in a restaurant we are working for a while to be able to leave Turkey I had to accept I nodded my head in agreement.

I was upset with my father why did he leave me in this country?! He knows my condition …why he didn't he do anything for me?! It's good to call him……..

Maybe his line will be controlled……. Maybe the police will find me………. I speak very briefly I just want to near his voice, that's all……..I'm worried about them.

I told Erdogan: I want a phone ……I have an urgent call.

Mikaeil said: who do you want to call?! It's dangerous!

Mikaeil, I'm worried…….there is no news about my father, it's impossible that he left me here ……….I just want to hear his voice, then I'll hang up the phone quickly.

Erdogan said: won't it cause trouble for me?

I said: no, be sure he gave me his mobile phone when I dialed the number, my hands were shaking and my heart was pounding.

All the cells in my body were excited after I dialed my heart beat slow down but I couldn't Breath all the cells in my body were waiting for a few words from the other side of the phone but when I heard a woman's voice I was disappointed "the mobile set, is off" I dialed again ……it was off.

This time I called my mother her mobile phone was off too I was very worried I called my father's house number.

Breath Hold

No one answered………I wanted to cry……..why am I un ware of everything?

Where is my daughter? Nahid……… sudden, Nahid's name to my mind ………I dialed Nahid's number ………again the same lady's voice ……."the mobile set is off."

I wanted to throw the phone on the ground God what happened to them?! Does that mean they were arrested them instead of me? No, it's impossible…….they can't do this ……I have to go back to Iran……..

I shouted to Mikaeil: I have to go back to Iran……….I have to hand myself over to the police.

Are you crazy?! Have you lost your mind?!

They arrested my family…….they arrested them instead of me……….

It's impossible……think about it…..call someone else……..

Noushin………I have to call her ……..she probably knows about them.

I hope that I remember her number ……..I remember that I bought this mobile number for her, wow, Farhad …….how good is this number………thank you, Farhad.

Noshin was like a sister for me she had a hard life before and I took care of her.

I dialed the number …….I heard the beep sound ……..my body was shaking …….after the third beep she answered ………..hello……..are you Noshin?

Yes that's me

Oh my God ………I wanted to scream and jump in the air.

I'm Farhad………..

Noshin screamed soloud that I was sure she was herself.

Breath Hold

Farhad ………..is it you?!………. Where are you?!

I felt a lump in my throat……..I asked hardly: I can't talk much just tell me, do you know about a week ago, Nahid called me and said that they are going to Turkey she called yesterday and said that they are in Istanbul. They are going to go to Germany in a few days.

I don't know how to Descible my condition ………..thank God………my family was in Istanbul………near me………

I could feel the smell of my daughter ………the lovely smell of my parents……..

I said to Noshin: please inform them in any way you can ……….

I'm in Zeytinburnu in Istanbul……….do you understand……..? Please inform them…..I'm waiting for them………

The last chapter

I stayed there for two days: My father could come after could come after me at any moment

Breath Hold

On the third day, I went to a restaurant with Mikaeil for work "waiting" is worse than "death" I told Hamed, if someone comes after me, give him the address of the restaurant.

The owner of the restaurant was a fat man he looked at me contemptuously he was from the Turkish Kurds he nodded his head in the affirmative.

Mikaeil said slowly: It means you have agreed to work here. Fist, we went to a room and changed our clothes all our clothes were blue then we went to the kitchen. A few other Iranians were also there.

Mikaeil took the broom and went inside the restaurant one of the Iranians pointed to the dishes and said: wash the dishes.

There was a lot of dishes black and crooked post and about 300 plates stacked on top of each other. Start with the post that we need the plates should be finished before noon.

I started washing the post no matter how much I washed they wouldn't get clean I don't know how long it took to wash the dishes I got tired and sat next to the wall I was hungry and I hadn't eaten anything since morning suddenly someone shouted badly damn ……are you sitting down?

When I looked, he was the owner of the restaurant who was pointing at me I didn't say anything I got up and looked for Mikaeil I wanted him to defend me, as if I couldn't do it myself but I didn't see Mikaeil I haven't see him since the morning when he went into the restaurant with a broom.

The same Iranian man told me: Go wash the toilets I looked at him and wanted to say that I'm not going, but I couldn't because I had no choice.

I had no strength and could hardly walk I went the toilets.

There were 6 toilets next to each other I wish they would give me some food, I was very hungry.

The cleaning equipment was in the corner of the bathroom it was hard work, but I had to endure.

Now that I'm not in prison and I wasn't executed it means that I have a "second chance"

I washed everything when the owner of the restaurant came in with his big belly I didn't took at him because I was getting angry I wanted to tear his big belly with a knife.

He looked at the first toilet and said: "it's dirty…… stupid man ……it's dirty…….

I got nervous and pummeled in his face.

His face was full of blood with his screams, with in a few seconds, everyone came there and beat me I felt like I was dying.

A little later, I felt that no one was hitting me……

Many be I was bead ……….I heard a familiar voice.

Breath Hold

Farhad……..

I opened my eyes hardly I saw my father. My eyes were closed again I heard his voice again: Farhad………Farhad……….

When I opened my eyes, my father was sitting in front of me. He hugged me and was crying ……….I was lying on the ground and I didn't understand anything I didn't know, if I was a sleep or a wake?

He shook me and called: Farhad …………Farhad

It was hard for me to believe I was crying he lifted me from the ground and sat me down.

I was staring at my father's face I still couldn't believe it I put my hand on his face to believe it.

He held my hand and kissed me several times I believed………..

We were both crying my father said: my son, I wish I were dead and didn't see you in this state.

He hugged me. I wanted to stay in his arms forever ………..

Now, 5 years have passed since that time and I live a Germany.

I divorced Nahid at the same time I couldn't bear her, but I told her that "you can stay here, just because you are my daughter's mother.

She returned to Iran and left Asal with me. I know she sacrificed I married with Sara and have another daughter I love my life.

I don't hate the word "love" anymore, because you can rebuild a life again.

The End.